Also by Luke Italiano

Geeky & Godly: Science Fiction, Fantasy, & Faith

Is it possible to be a geek and a Christian?

Can you be a fangirl and still love Jesus?

Spoiler Alert: Yes. Yes, you can!

Ages 10+

The Broken Prophet: Elijah's Story

Fed by ravens; living among foreign, unfaithful people.

Rejoice with Elijah as God sends fire from the sky on Mount Caramel.

Mourn with him as he wanders the desert alone.

See how God cares for his broken prophet.

Biblical Fiction

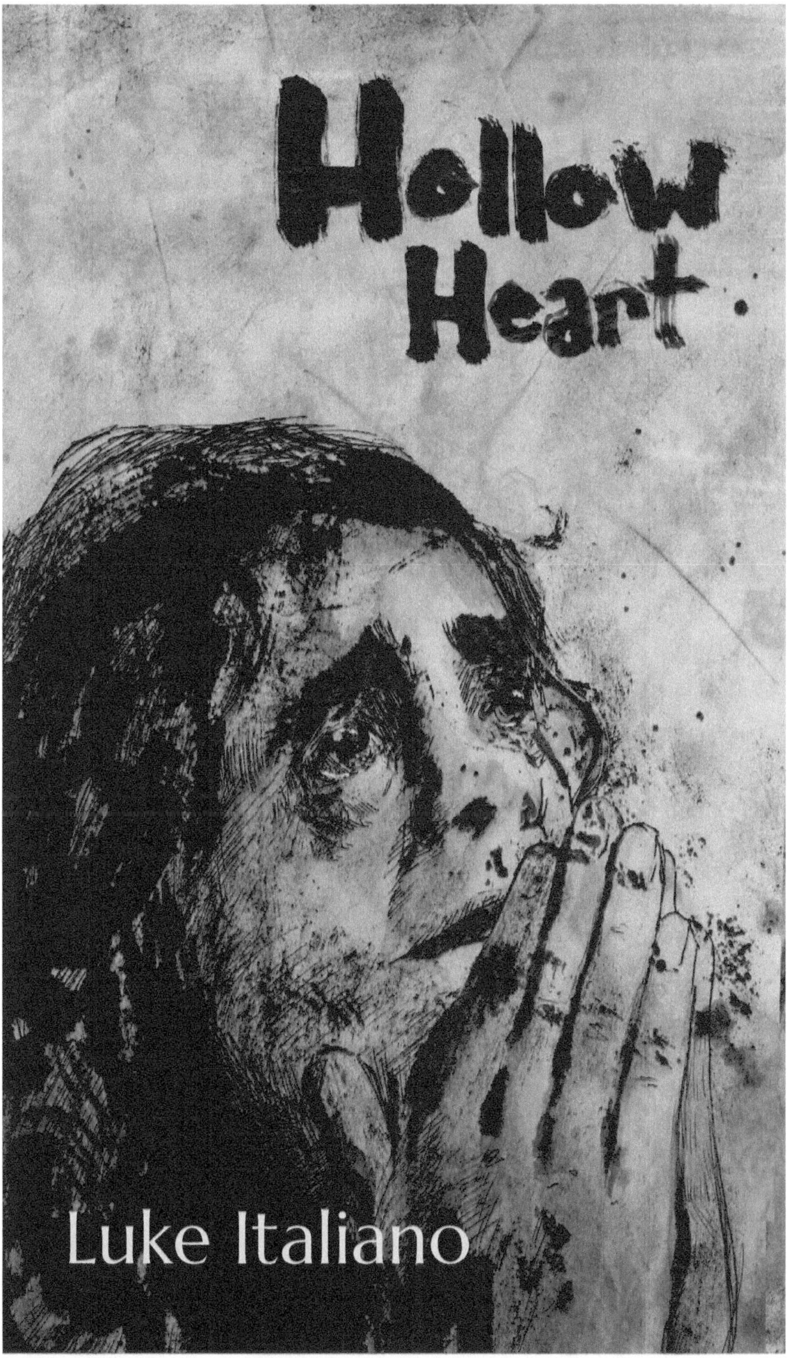
Hollow
Heart
Luke Italiano

Cover art by Maida Jaspersen

Published by Dawnsbrook Waters an imprint of Dawnsbrook Press

dawnsbrook.com

Psalm 13

1 How long, O LORD? Will you forget me forever?
   How long will you hide your face from me?
2 How long must I experience worries in my soul,
   sorrow in my heart every day?
   How long will my enemy tower over me?

3 Look at me. Answer me, O LORD my God.
   Give light to my eyes
      so I do not sleep in death,
4   so my enemy does not say, "I have overcome him,"
      so my foes do not rejoice when I fall.

5 But I trust in your mercy.
   My heart rejoices in your salvation.
6 I will sing to the LORD
      because he has accomplished his purpose for me.

Special Thanks to:

The brothers of the Ohio Conference of the Michigan District,
who heard an early form of this book.

All the brothers who participated in my informal survey,
for sharing their thoughts and experiences of depression with me.

Table of Contents

Responding to Depression

DEVOTIONS FOR THOSE WITH DEPRESSION

Introduction

I have depression. Which really means that depression has me. It owns me.

Thursday. I wanted to do nothing. A pressure pushed down on my neck and back, bending me over. Breathing became toil. My Bride looked at my expression and knew: Today was a bad day.

I didn't call up the friendly neighborhood depression salesman and say, "Yeah, Thursday? Could you stop by? I'm a little low on purposeless gloom." And it's not even that I forgot to pay the happyman. "Oh, sorry, I didn't send the check for my monthly supply of glee. Can I make up the difference on next month's bill?"

Nope. Depression owns me. And Thursday it decided it would be nice to pay a visit to its little slave and maybe hang around for a while. Make sure I didn't think it was ignoring me.

But I'm a Christian. OK, I'm not supposed to be a grinning idiot at all times. I'm not some megapreacher that always has to look smarmy. I get that. Sadness is a part of being Christian. Jeremiah wrote Lamentations. Martha mourned at the grave of her brother. Christians suffer. It's part of who we are.

But shouldn't I have joy, no matter my emotion at the moment? Isn't that what Paul said? "Rejoice in the Lord always! I say it again: Rejoice!"

Oh, never mind. It's depression. We'll just snuff out that joy. Can't have that around.

It's like I suddenly lose the ability to even fake a smile. I lose the ability to care. I can go through the motions of what I need to do, but there's no will behind it. In case you're wondering, that kind of depression can be hell on most people. For a pastor who's supposed to be happy to see people? Yeah, not so good.

> *Depression makes me realize how little I am. How small and broken and insignificant.*

It's supposed to be better than this. I have my joy! You can't take this joy from me!

And the depression mocks me. It plucks the joy from between my hands. It swallows whatever light I have.

Depression owns me.

Today was a good day, but even thinking about it brings me down. I can feel my face taking that slack expression. All the muscle tension vanishes. It really feels like my heart is lowering. I just don't care.

Why should I? If I can't even hold on to the joy that Christ gives me, if that treasure is so easily plucked away, what else could possibly matter?

I'm not good enough to hold on to his gifts. I'm not strong enough. I'm weak. And now the depression makes me realize how little I am. How small and broken and insignificant. Pastor in a failing church. Want to know why it's failing? Look in a mirror, little man. If you gave your best, maybe, maybe it would be good enough. But let's be honest: You don't do that. You're not good enough.

It's just one more failure in the string of your life. You wandered through your schooling; you never conquered it. It's sheer luck you married at all, much less such an amazing woman. She deserves so much better. You're not good enough for her. She should have a real man. And all that crap in high school? If your congregation knew the truth about you, about who you really are, they'd drive you out.

2

And they'd be right to do it.

And now I'm lying on my side, without even the will to pull up into the fetal position. I'm done. Depression owns me, and it's having its way. I'm not strong enough to hold on to the joy that Jesus gives. What right do I have to fight back at all? Let it ravage my heart and all that lies within me. I won't fight.

I know in my head that it's the depression. That it's making me look at things this way. That it's turning my head to make me see only one side of anything. I know all this in my head, but it does not change the weight on my heart.

Because I cannot hold on to the joy that Jesus gives.

But Jesus holds me.

Depression tries to enslave me. But Jesus owns me. He paid for me with blood and suffering and death. He has paid a dear price. What has depression paid to own me? Nothing.

I do not belong to depression. I have depression. Jesus has me. This is the way of things.

All those failures? They are mine. I am a failure. I am a broken man. I am so little. I wear such shabby rags when I parade around in my accomplishments.

But Jesus has given me a new record. He dresses me in a gleaming robe of righteousness. And I am not good enough for it. He wastes it on a nobody like me. And yet, he lavishes me with his love. With the honor he has earned. He gives me his record of success. Of conquering the sins I have rolled around in.

He makes me whole.

Look, this does not mean that I am now grinning like an idiot. It means that I am not alone in my suffering. It does not mean every problem is solved. It means that it's not my job to find the solution.

I have depression. Jesus has me.

I still hurt. That void continues. But the void is a lie. I am still a failure, but that is not the end of my story. Because Jesus has made me something different. If my congregation knew everything about me, every sin of my past, every thought I allow in my sinful nature? Yeah. My ministry could well be over.

But I have been made new. And I long for the day that it's all over. I yearn to get rid of these stupid lies that live within me, that worm their way through my heart and lay such hollow eggs to leave me empty. I long for the place where there is no need for broken shepherds to limp as they attempt to tend the sheep. Oh, to lay under the hand of the Shepherd. To know—to know in ways I cannot fathom now—that all is good, that my Shepherd loves me even in my pain, even in my hurt, that I am not alone, that these lies are lies, and to know that not only in my head, but to laugh at the sheer ludicrousness of what they claim.

And this is the struggle I have. On days like Thursday, when depression tells me lies that I believe even when I know they are wrong.

On Thursday, I visited a standing appointment with a family that has struggled with depression. And I told them flat-out: I was having a bad day.

They didn't know I had depression. And when they found out: There was no judgment. There was no unwelcome hug. They simply understood. They shared my sorrow.

Oh, God is so good. Even in the midst of such pain, to show his love through others. To show that though we are broken, though we are so shattered, he loves us in our greatest shames and our secret sins and yes, even in our depression. We are not alone.

And he himself knows every grief. He wept when he was here. He does not hold us as someone who does not understand. Our Brother has not forgotten his sojourn here. Oh, Christian, do you see? He does not take away your sorrow, because he walks with you in it. Because he wishes to show you that his love is real, whether or not you feel it. Because he wants to point you beyond the pain of today, to the cross, to the proof that he has not forgotten.

This pain is good. My depression is a gift. It forces me to say that yes, my strength is not in me. And I cannot hold on to any joy.

But joy holds on to me.

My Jesus holds me in his hands, and none can move me from his grasp. Not because I hold on to him, but because he holds on to the one he has bled for. And my brokenness points me to that assurance.

> *God is so good.*
> *Even in the midst of*
> *such pain—we are*
> *not alone*

I am a Christian. I have depression. Jesus has me.

I WROTE THAT JOURNAL entry on January 31, 2015. It presents a normal reality for who I am and what I struggle with.

In March 2014, I experienced a difficult time of ministry. The circumstances . . . really don't matter much anymore, other than to say there were exterior pressures that I am told were greater than normal for most ministries. One day I couldn't get out of bed. It wasn't that I was too tired. It wasn't that I had nothing to do. I had work to do, and I was rested. I could not physically move myself from the bed. And that's when I knew I had to get some sort of help.

By March 30th, I had an initial diagnosis of depression and possible bipolar disorder from my family physician; she recommended I see a specialist for a more solid diagnosis. I considered leaving the ministry immediately. How could a pastor have bipolar disorder? I had served enough people who struggled with it. Can you imagine what would happen if a pastor was called to console the mourning while he was having a manic episode?

At the same time, I felt relief. The demon that plagued me had a name. The darkness had a designation. And now that it had a designation, perhaps it could be fought. I began counseling with a pastor to address my depression.

On May 4th, I received an official diagnosis: clinical depression, not bipolar. The doctor told me that meds were optional. I struggled with whether or not to take them. Should a pastor rely on medications in that way? I'll address the subject later, but for now, I can say that I initially declined medication, though now I take some.

Meanwhile, the counseling helped. Immensely.

And the reason it helped . . . was that it took me to Jesus. It helped me identify the lies my heart spoke. It helped me see the deceits I had trusted. It took me to the truth.

The truth that Jesus has already won the fight. That Jesus loves me. That he is not ashamed of me. That he claims me. That he forgives me.

That it is not my burden to carry.

I have depression. Jesus has me.

This book will demonstrate that depression is nothing new. It will introduce several causes as well as some of the effects of depression. It will give some advice on how to handle depression and some encouragement as well.

My friend, I hope you don't share my struggle. It is not one I would wish on you. If you do suffer from depression, I hope this book provides tools to help. If you don't experience these kinds of lows, my hope is that this book will help you understand and equip you to help others bear their burdens when they need your help. For all, I pray that God uses this book to deepen your praise of the God who loves us in every shame.

Understanding Depression

Taking a closer look at depression—what causes it, what it looks like, what it is, and what it isn't. Seeking to gain a deeper understanding of depression, whether in ourselves or in others.

Chapter 1

Shouldn't I Be Happy?

BUT . . . I'M A CHRISTIAN, aren't I? Shouldn't I be happy? Jesus died for me. He took my sins away. I have eternal life. Depression shouldn't affect me at all! Not if I have enough faith. Not if everything I believe is true. Christians shouldn't have depression!

Let me laugh for a moment.

Look, the Gospel gives joy. It really does. Paul says, "Rejoice in the Lord always! I will say it again: Rejoice!"[1] We are freed from our sins. We are made children of God. We have a home in heaven. These are real. And yes, the response to all this is joy.

But joy is not the same thing as happiness.

Joy is a reaction to reality. We are saved. Jesus has died for us. Nothing can change these facts. Nothing can shake what is real. Joy is a fruit of the Spirit and grows through the Gospel. In other words, we're like trees. If you want a tree to produce fruit, you've got to water it. Do you want joy fruit in your life? You've got to be watered with the truth that there is no condemnation for you because Jesus was condemned in your place. That's the only way to have joy. Again, joy is a reaction to reality.

---

1. Philippians 4:4

Happiness is a reaction to circumstances. That smile you feel when things are going well? That's happiness. It's not a sin. Praise God for the gift of happiness![2] But nowhere does God tell us to go around grinning like idiots. If he had, Jesus himself would have sinned.[3] Remember, Jesus wept[4] and he knew grief.[5]

It is possible to know joy and not feel happy. It is also possible to feel happy and not know joy. Proverbs expresses that thought well: "Even in laughter a heart can ache, and the end of joy may be grief."[6] The first time I struggled with depression, this verse helped me so, so much. Yes, I can smile and still hurt. Yes, I can laugh and still be in emotional pain. I'm not lying to my friends. I'm simply experiencing two emotions at the same time.

> *Happiness is a reaction to circumstances. Joy is a reaction to reality.*

Does being a Christian mean I need to be happy—or at least fake happiness? Not at all. There are some times that we need to control our emotions. For instance, if your friend suffers a great grief, it's good to dampen any happiness you might feel at that moment so you can weep with those who weep.[7] That said, I'd argue that "faking happiness" at least approaches giving false testimony about ourselves. We want to speak the

---

2. Ecclesiastes 5:19
3. John 13:21, for instance.
4. John 11:35
5. Isaiah 53:3
6. Proverbs 14:13
7. Romans 12:15

truth in love, and that love may mean setting aside emotions for a short time, but we don't want to deceive. So please, don't "fake happiness." In the end, it'll hurt you.

And there can be a huge pressure to fake happiness, especially on Sunday mornings.

"Hey! How're you doing?"

"Fine!"

It's the most-told lie in my experience. No, I'm not fine, but I don't want to admit it. I don't want you to know. After all, if you knew, you'd judge me. Church is a place for happy people, which means I need to at least pretend to be happy when I'm here.

If you feel pressure to always look happy on Sunday mornings, let me release that pressure for you: If it's okay for Jesus, it's okay for you. Jesus wept. He didn't always smile. Sometimes the people around us—and we ourselves—need that reminder. It's not a sin to hurt. It's not a sin to not be happy. It's not your job to always be okay.

As Christians, we are simply to show Jesus. Even and especially in weakness, let others see Jesus. If Paul was a broken jar,[8] you are no less than he.

And when you're open with your pain, something amazing happens. You give permission for the people around you to be honest with their hurts, too. They get permission to be broken.

And only the broken find comfort in Jesus.

---

8. 2 Corinthians 4:7

Chapter 2

Depression Isn't New

I TOOK AN INFORMAL survey of a number of pastors. I asked participants if they thought any people in the Bible had depression. I received responses that included Moses, Gideon, David, Elijah, Jeremiah, Peter, Thomas, and Paul.[9]

I'm not sure if I agree with the assessments of all of those, but each person a pastor suggested did encounter difficult situations, and they certainly didn't always face them with a smile.

Moses limped through the desert. The most powerful man in the world wanted him dead. He fled all he had known. Friends? Family? Power? All gone. The sun burned his eyes. The sand scorched his skin. Still, he plodded through the wilderness.

And then he found a shred of happiness. A desert tribe welcomed him in. He found a wife. When she gave birth to his son, he named the baby Gershom "for he said, 'I have become an alien in a foreign land.' "[10]

He mourned what he had lost. He looked around at the blessings God had given, and he felt bitterness. This wasn't what he'd planned on.

And then his life got worse.

---

9. Luke Italiano, "Depression in the Ministry Survey," Conducted March–April 2018.
10. Exodus 2:22

God sent him home again to lead his people out of slavery. Moses saw success for a short season. With a mighty hand, God led the people out of Egypt. Finally, the nightmare was over.

But then the people complained. They rebelled. They refused to follow Moses. As a result, God said they would all die, and only their children would enter the Promised Land. For forty years,

> *God told us about the tears.*
> *He told us about the pain.*
> *He told us about the wounds.*

Moses wandered the desert. For forty years, he saw everyone he knew die far from their promised home.

During that time, Moses wrote Psalm 90. It's not a song that brims over with jubilation. No. It breathes weariness!

Did Moses suffer from depression? I can't say that he did, but I wouldn't be surprised. The Bible describes a difficult life and a man familiar with suffering. At least at times, he gave in to bitterness.

And what about the hero Gideon? If you know his story, you might recall his triumph. God led him into battle with only three hundred soldiers against an army of 135,000.[11] That's what I remember most about him from Sunday school. God used him to bring a glorious victory!

But that's not where we meet him. Before that victory, he was hiding. He took what little grain his family had and threshed it in a pit. The Angel of the LORD visited him. "The LORD is with you, mighty warrior!"

---

11. Judges 8:10

And Gideon gives a bitter laugh. "If the LORD is with us, why has all this happened? The LORD has forsaken us."

Abandoned. Rejected.

Yeah, I can't say for sure that Gideon had depression, but that reaction could easily be expressed by someone struggling with depression.

Peter, leader of the early church, experienced strong emotions, flipping quickly between anger,[12] confidence,[13] and sorrow.[14] Those may be signs of a person struggling with manic depression. At the very least, we can say he experienced emotions in a deep, loud way. I grew up as a German Lutheran. We're not exactly known for our emotional eloquence. Peter always seemed strange to me. What man would be that loud with his emotions? Well, now I know. Plenty of men express their emotions loudly in healthy ways. Peter, though . . . Maybe he experienced depression.

They wanted Jesus dead. It was a public secret. The religious leaders in Jerusalem wanted his blood.

And then Jesus did the unthinkable. He resolutely set out for Jerusalem. His followers didn't know what to do. Why would he do this? It's insane! Who would willingly march toward the home of his enemies?

And Thomas, the same one who would doubt Jesus was alive Easter evening, said, "Let's go too, so that we may die with him."[15]

---

12. John 18:10
13. Matthew 26:33
14. Mark 14:72
15. John 11:16

Again, I don't know whether Thomas suffered depression, but that resignation toward death? It could be a sign of depression.

Paul wrote half of the New Testament. He traveled the world and planted dozens of churches. Yet he himself struggled with melancholy and despaired of his own life.[16]

Look, I don't know if any of these people had depression. I don't know what a modern diagnosis might reveal. What I can say is that they struggled. I know they experienced melancholy. God could have just ignored those dark parts of their lives. He could've presented a sterilized Sunday school lesson which said everyone was always happy—except maybe when things got bad for a little bit, but they still knew God was in charge.

But God didn't tell us that.

He told us about the tears. He told us about the pain. He told us about the wounds.

So no, I don't know that any of these people had depression, but I know that they weren't "just fine." They weren't always happy.

And that means they were a lot like me.

I'd like to spend a little more time with three particular people who struggled like I do with depression. And if you've got depression, I'm guessing that you'll identify with them, too.

---

16. 2 Corinthians 1:8

Chapter 3

David's Depression

FIRST, CONSIDER THE WORDS of King David:
Psalm 13

    1 How long, O LORD? Will you forget me forever?
      How long will you hide your face from me?
    2 How long must I experience worries in my soul,
      sorrow in my heart every day?
      How long will my enemy tower over me?

    3 Look at me. Answer me, O LORD my God.
      Give light to my eyes
         so I do not sleep in death,
    4   so my enemy does not say, "I have overcome him,"
      so my foes do not rejoice when I fall.

    5 But I trust in your mercy.
      My heart rejoices in your salvation.
    6 I will sing to the LORD
         because he has accomplished his purpose for me.

Will you forget me forever? You're gone! My heart is hollow. It's echoing with the screams of my pain. Sorrow drowns me. God, where are you? Why are you ignoring me? You promised! *You promised!* You said you were Immanuel. You said you were "God with us!"

Maybe you're "with us," but you're not with *me*. I can't find you. You've forgotten me.

When my heart echoes with the sounds of my sorrow, this is the psalm that brings me most comfort. The Bible is not all sunshine and smiles. Here is a man who knows what it is to struggle with himself, even as outside forces press in. This isn't just some passage that describes what David's going through, though. This shows how any Christian can struggle with depression. I've used this in devotions so many times. This psalm declares, "You are not alone!"

> *God says, "Come to me. Pour out your heart. I am big enough to take your pain."*

David's honest with his emotions. He doesn't tell himself to cheer up. He doesn't count his blessings. He doesn't give himself any kind of shallow platitudes like "it's going to be okay." He doesn't say, "Well, God promised that all things will work out for my best, so I can get through this!" He doesn't act as if everything's fine. He admits the darkness that he experiences.

Can you cry out like that? David utters heresy! How can he say God's forgotten him? The Father turned his back on Jesus, but never on David! But in our pain, we can forget, and in our sorrow, we cry out. God does not smite David for his misery. Instead, he records it for us. He says, "Come to me. Pour out your heart. I am big enough to take your pain." So yes. Admit your struggles.

Oh, this is so, so hard in our culture. We think we need to pretend that everything's "just fine." That's why there are so many filters on our phones. They're not just for fun. They're created so we can make our--

selves look better in some way. Sillier. Prettier. More fun. We dare not reveal how wounded we truly are.

But God didn't filter David's words. He used David's darkness to show us that we can bring our darkness to him. "God speaks through [the psalms] at the level of giving us words for the times when we lack them. They effectively say, it is OK to say these things to me."[17]

> Instead of just praising God, David took time to explain his fear and sorrow with utter clarity, allowing readers to say, "Oh! Me too!" David showed us that he understood despair and loss, and this helps us trust him when he went on to claim that God had restored his soul. Without his raw insights on suffering and fear, his joy wouldn't ring as true – the inclusion of both helps us transition from paralysis to praise.[18]

The psalm is only six verses long. For four of those verses, David cries out in anguish. And for two verses . . .

Well, look at those last two verses. Is it a happy ending?

When I read those verses, I hear David clinging to God's promises. He sings through gritted teeth, with tears streaming down his face, "God, I know what you've promised! I know who you are! You rejoice in mercy! Your love never fails! I *know* this is true, even when I can't see it. Even when my heart is hollow, yours is full of love. Even now, even now in this sorrow, I rejoice. You've saved me. It's true. I can't see how, I can't understand how, but I know that even now you are *good*. Even in this darkness, you accomplish your purpose for me."

---

17. Mark Meynell, *When Darkness Seems My Closest Friend* (London: Inter-Varsity Press, 2018), 36.
18. Rebecca K. Reynolds, *Courage, Dear Heart* (Colorado Springs, CO: NavPress, 2018), 11.

David turns not to his emotions, but to what he knows is true. He cries out, finding comfort in God's unfailing love. He looks forward to singing to the Lord again, because he has always been good to him.

And this is what we can do. When our hearts echo with the sounds of our anguish, we can start by being honest with our struggles. No, don't wallow. That's not what I mean. But we bring our pleas before a God we know is good. We carry to him the heart he already purchased from death.

And we say, "Lord, you are good, even now. I know you love me. Here. I cry out to you. You have not abandoned me. You forsook your only Son instead of turning your back on me. I know you won't forget me now."

If you struggle with depression, I highly recommend committing this psalm, Psalm 13, to memory. Bookmark it in your Bible or on your phone. Reread it when you feel down.

You are not alone. God recorded David's plea. Here is someone who understands, and this was a man after God's own heart. God loved David dearly. Do you think he would love you any less because you struggle the same way?

It's okay to be honest with your struggle. Your salvation is not dependent on your emotions. Your salvation is secure in Jesus.

Chapter 4

Elijah's Depression

ELIJAH FELT THE HEAT of the flames against his face. The people declared, "The LORD, he is God!"[19]

He'd won. He'd finally, finally won.

God had used him to declare judgment on King Ahab. For more than three years, there'd been no rain. And for more than three years, Elijah had hidden away. He'd watched the nation he loved fall further and further away from the God who is faithful to every promise. He'd witnessed his nation suffer more and more because of their stubbornness.

During that time, God had provided a widow to take care of Elijah. God had used miracles to provide for Elijah and the widow's family. And then Elijah had cried out in despair when the widow's son died. "O LORD, my God, have you sent tragedy on this woman with whom I am staying by killing her son?"[20] And do you see God's response? He didn't yell at Elijah. He didn't command Elijah to just get over it. He didn't tell Elijah to cheer up. He didn't even suggest that if Elijah had more faith, things would work out better. Instead, God graciously raised the widow's son to life.

19. 1 Kings 18:38–39
20. 1 Kings 17:20

After three and a half years of exile, Elijah returned to prove that the God he served was indeed real. The people joined him after the great victory at Mount Carmel. Rain finally fell from what had been a barren sky.

It was over. The long night was finally, finally over.

Three years of pain, of fear, roll off Elijah's shoulders as he lifts his face to accept the rain.

And then the queen vows revenge. And Elijah runs. Suddenly, it is over. Any hope he had vanishes.

His hollow heart screams out pain.

Elijah wanders into the wilderness. His feet take him south. And far away from anyone who could see his woundedness, he prays to die. With that prayer on his lips, he falls asleep.

Now God doesn't command Elijah to get his act together. God doesn't tell Elijah to cheer up. Instead, he sends an angel. He provides food and water for the journey ahead.

Elijah eats and drinks, and then he goes right back to sleep.

The angel comes back. He wakes Elijah again. He provides.

And then Elijah sets out. For forty days he stumbles deeper and deeper into the wastes, farther and farther south.

These are not the actions of a believer who has it all together. These are the actions of a man deep in depression. He knows how broken the world is. He feels alone. He feels like he is the last. And like so many people who struggle with depression, Elijah retreats from the world.

> *God allowed Elijah to struggle with depression. He allowed his prophet time to heal.*

And God lets him.

God doesn't turn him around. He gives Elijah room in his despair. God gives him more than a month so he can be alone, so he can process everything that has happened. God never commands Elijah to smile or buck up. He never promises that everything will turn out all right or that it will all be okay. God gives Elijah one of the best gifts for someone with depression: time.

And in the end, God tells Elijah he is not alone.

He's not alone.

Those in depression are convinced they are alone. I've been there. I've felt that isolation. Yes, I knew intellectually that there were more people around me, that they loved me, but in the moment, those things didn't matter. I could only hear the echoes of my own pain.

But God comes alongside us with comfort.

He allowed Elijah to struggle with depression. He allowed his prophet time to heal. And then he offered real comfort: "No, Elijah, you are not alone. I have preserved thousands more. Your isolation is at an end."

He gave Elijah new marching orders. They included a command which showed Elijah wouldn't be the last prophet. A man named Elisha would follow him.[21]

So if you struggle with depression, take comfort in how God treats Elijah. God treats you the same way.

It's okay to take time to take care of yourself. You cannot serve oth-

---

21. 1 Kings 19:17

ers if you're falling apart. If you need time alone to be healthy, then spend time alone. This is necessary time for you. God commanded that we watch out for the bodies of those around us. It's not just "don't murder" but show love by taking care of their bodies, too.

And that commandment covers your body, too.

Elijah returned from his journey. He got back to work.

And at the end of his life, God chose to take him directly to heaven. He never died.

Consider that: the prophet we most easily identify as struggling with depression is the same prophet God took directly to heaven.

Your depression does not lock you out of heaven. Your depression may tell you that you must earn God's love. Your depression may tell you that you are not loved. Your depression may tell you that you are alone.

Your depression lies.

Jesus himself chose to come to earth to save *you*. Not just the rest of the world. Not just the people around you. You. No, you are not worthy of such love. Neither are the people who don't have depression. So what? This is love: not that we have loved God, but that he loved us and sent his Son to be the atoning sacrifice for our sins.[22] For you.

> *Your depression may tell you that you are not loved, that you are alone.*
>
> *Your depression lies.*

---

22. 1 John 4:10

Chapter 5

Jeremiah's Depression

JEREMIAH WEPT.

14 May the day I was born be cursed.
Do not let the day my mother gave birth to me be blessed.
15 May the man be cursed who brought news to my father,
"A son is born to you,"
the man who brought him great joy.
16 Let that man be like the cities the LORD overthrew
without pity.
Let him hear a cry in the morning,
an alarm for war at noon,
17 because he did not put me to death in the womb,
so that my mother would have been my grave,
and her womb would have been pregnant forever.
18 Why did I emerge from that womb
to see trouble and sorrow,
to finish my days in shame?[23]

What could lead a prophet to cry out like that? Read that poetry again out loud. Let the syllables echo. Here is anguish. Here is pain.

Jeremiah called out warning after warning. Come back! Repent!

His people ignored him.

---

23. Jeremiah 20:14–18

He raged. He wept. He prophesied. He spoke God's own word to them.

The king threatened him to shut him up. Messages like Jeremiah's were bad for morale, after all. He imprisoned Jeremiah. He cut up Jeremiah's messages and burned them. Anything to silence the prophet.

Jeremiah pleaded for his people to turn from their wicked ways. They had rejected God. They had turned from his promises. The God of grace wasn't good enough for them.

And then all the warnings came true. Babylon sent its army to Jerusalem.

> *Sometimes people think if they had worked harder, more faithfully, just believed more, maybe it wouldn't be this way.*
>
> *But you cannot escape the pit your heart has dug for you that way.*

Jeremiah cried out again. And again.

Still he was told to be quiet.

And Jerusalem fell. Jeremiah watched as the walls were broken. He heard the cries of children as the Babylonian army crushed them. He smelled the blood that smeared the walls. He felt the heat of the flames as the temple itself was destroyed.

It wasn't the end, though. Those that survived? The Babylonians led them away into captivity. They were marched out of the city, never to see their homes again. Jeremiah wasn't important enough to be carried away. The Babylonians left him behind.

Is it any wonder that Jeremiah's known as the weeping prophet?

Once more read that chunk of Jeremiah's book. Hear the anguish.

Sobs wrack his body. He can barely wheeze any breath into his lungs. His despair lays thick on him.

The prophet vents his full frustration to God. He would rather not live than face what he faces. The images he has seen are seared into his mind, so even when he closes his eyes, he can see destruction.

He'd warned them.

If only they'd listened. If only he had tried harder. Maybe he could have done more. And so he expresses shame. He wants to hide. He sees only his failures. He feels that's all anyone sees when they look at him. And can you blame him? He'd been told to shut up for years. He hadn't. But still, his words weren't enough.

And if you have any doubt that Jeremiah experienced depression, go read Lamentations. These are the words of a devastated man, bitter words from a bitter heart.

Once more, God doesn't hide this bitterness. He puts it on display for us. And what does he show us?

Faithfulness doesn't mean a person can escape depression. Sometimes people in depression feel that their emotional state is their own fault. If they had worked harder, more faithfully, found better ways to work around things, just believed more, maybe it wouldn't be this way. It's so stupid. They should know better by now. They want to hide. Let darkness swallow them so no one can look on them ever again.

You cannot escape the pit your heart has dug for you. Do not fall for that variation of the theology of glory.

The theology of glory describes the belief that if you really have faith, if you give to God, your life will be easy. Sure, there may be some hardship here or there, but as long as you believe, things will generally get better. It is perhaps the most dangerous heresy ever created.

"If you believe, your life will be easy"? That just means that you're working your way to heaven. You're not depending on God. You're depending on you, the strength of your own faith. And you know, don't you? You know you're not strong enough.

"If you believe, your life will be easy"? Jeremiah believed. His life wasn't easy. What about the apostle Paul? That was a faithful man, yet he died in prison. How about any of the apostles? Lives of pain.

Oh, and what about Jesus?

Your faithfulness does not mean you will have an easy life. Not at all.

You may be faithful. You may speak God's Word with passion. You may strive to love your Savior and your neighbor with all that is in you. And yet, you may experience rejection. Pain. Depression.

The world is broken. Your body may be broken in a way that causes you to have depression. You may react to the circumstances around you with dismay. Perhaps you live in the ruins of a life wrecked by your own sin.

But take heart. Courage, dear one. Jeremiah wasn't saved because of his faithfulness. He wasn't saved because of the people he spoke to. He wasn't saved by clinging to an undying optimism or a practical level-headedness.

He was saved because of God's faithfulness to him.

Chapter 6

Depression Is Real

As I LOOK BACK on the people the Bible tells us about, I see depression. Maybe you don't. I've heard Elijah's time in the desert described as a "pity party." I personally find that description more than a little dismissive. I mean, Elijah went from glorious victory to utter defeat in the course of . . . what? A day? But then again, maybe it wasn't depression. Maybe Elijah should have just stood his ground and he would have been fine.

Certainly my history of struggling with my own depression colors how I view certain biblical narratives. I think we could have an honest debate about whether or not people back then would have fit modern diagnoses. After all, God has not told us in his Word whether any of the historical accounts include depression.

That said, don't think that we can debate whether or not depression is a real thing.

It's not merely "feeling down" or having a bad day. I think we've all had those moments. Maybe it's Monday. You come back to work after a great weekend, and no one's in a good mood. The boss is harsh. You just don't feel great. You come home simply defeated. Those days come. And yes, they stink. That's not what depression is, though.

I'm not using depression as an excuse to sit around all day, either. Frankly, this is one of those things I hate the most. When depression hits me, I can't get out of bed. If I do get out of bed, I can't concentrate. If I force myself to concentrate somehow, the depression strikes back twice as hard. I have things to do. I can't just sit around. And yet, the depression won't let me move. So trust me, it's not laziness. Could depression become an excuse for laziness? Sure. But that's not what depression is.

Depression isn't just a symptom of a weak will. Jeremiah spoke God's Word against impossible odds. He had a strong will, determination, and discipline. He didn't crumble under pressure. And yet, read Lamentations.

> *When I suffer depression, I think it's only because I'm lazy. I'm weak. It's just a bad day. Get over it. I had therapy for this! I should know better!*

The problem is, all of these thoughts about depression swirl around my head constantly. When I suffer depression, I think it's only because I'm lazy. I'm weak. It's just a bad day. Get over it. I had therapy for this! I should know better!

When I first realized I needed to get help, I feared for my ministry. Was it possible for a man with depression to lead God's flock? I didn't doubt my abilities. Nothing in me had changed; I had simply come to the realization I needed help. But there's a certain stigma about depression. Would my fellow ministers push me out? Would they think I was unreliable? Would I be accused of being too weak? Would someone argue that I just needed to "deal with it"? Would congregation members use it as an excuse to ignore me when I spoke God's Word?

I am thankful that, in my case, I received nothing but support from my fellow pastors. If the brothers thought I wasn't worthy of the ministry, they kept their thoughts to themselves. In fact, a few even said I was brave to go get help. I don't think I was brave. I simply admitted I needed help.

But that fear is still there: The thought that someone might think depression isn't real. The possibility that what I suffer is all in my head. I admit that I get defensive about it at times.

Let me say it again: Depression isn't just feeling sad or being lazy. Depression is real. Mayo Clinic defines depression this way:

> Depression is a mood disorder that causes a persistent feeling of sadness and loss of interest. Also called major depressive disorder or clinical depression, it affects how you feel, think and behave and can lead to a variety of emotional and physical problems. You may have trouble doing normal day-to-day activities, and sometimes you may feel as if life isn't worth living.

> *But depression is real. It isn't a weakness, and you can't simply "snap out" of it.*

More than just a bout of the blues, depression isn't a weakness and you can't simply "snap out" of it. Depression may require long-term treatment. But don't get discouraged. Most people with depression feel better with medication, psychotherapy or both.[24]

In my case, it was relatively simple to verify I wasn't just being lazy or blue. A blood test verified I had next to no vitamin D.

24. Mayo Clinic Staff, "Depression (major depressive disorder)," Mayo Clinic, February 3, 2018, https://www.mayoclinic.org/diseases-conditions/depression/symptoms-causes/syc-20356007.

Low levels of vitamin D have been linked with depression.[25] What I experienced in my depression was real, caused in part by this vitamin deficiency. No amount of positive thinking or pushing through it would ever balance out the levels of vitamin D I needed.

Depression is real. It can be debilitating. And no one has really nailed down all the causes.

---

25. Dale Archer, "Vitamin D Deficiency and Depression," Psychology Today, July 11, 2013, https://www.psychologytoday.com/us/blog/reading-between-the-headlines/201307/vitamin-d-deficiency-and-depression.
This article includes numerous links to related articles for more information.

Chapter 7

Causes of Depression

HARVARD HEALTH REPORTS:

It's often said that depression results from a chemical imbalance, but that figure of speech doesn't capture how complex the disease is. Research suggests that depression doesn't spring from simply having too much or too little of certain brain chemicals. Rather, there are many possible causes of depression, including faulty mood regulation by the brain, genetic vulnerability, stressful life events, medications, and medical problems. It's believed that several of these forces interact to bring on depression.[26]

As noted by Harvard Health, there are many causes of depression. I'd like to suggest four major causes of depression:

- ☐ Medical causes
- ☐ The effects of sin
- ☐ The sin of others
- ☐ My own sin

These four causes interact, as noted in the quote above. While it's true that some depression is "merely" medical, for many, there is a mix

---

26. "What Causes Depression?," Harvard Health, last modified January 10, 2022, https://www.health.harvard.edu/mind-and-mood/what-causes-depression.

of factors that may cause depression. And identifying and addressing all of them takes both skill and patience.

Medical problems might cause hormonal imbalances. Some medications can lead to depression. It's outside the purview of this book to go into all the medical jargon, except to say that some causes of depression are purely medical.[27] These causes mean that depression cannot simply be treated with a positive attitude; depression is as serious and as real as a broken leg. Some depression must be treated medically. Should a Christian get medical help for their depression? We'll address that matter directly later, but the short answer is: yes.

However, for most cases, if depression is handled purely medically, only some of the causes will be addressed.

We live in a broken world. The effects of sin are evident everywhere. Sin brings with it death. Death brings separation. The soul separates from the body. Loved ones are forced apart. The woman who has been married for decades may well experience depression as a result of this separation when her husband dies.

> *In our broken world, there are many factors that may interact to cause depression.*

When Mary and Martha mourned the death of their brother, Jesus didn't tell them to cheer up. He understood that this broken world brings pain. He mourned with them.[28]

---

27. I highly recommend the chapter on depressive disorders in *A Christian Guide to Mental Illness Volume 1* by Stephen M. Saunders as a good place to get some basic knowledge about depression from a solid, Christian source.

28. John 11

It's not just death, though. Relationships end, and not always for sinful reasons. Sometimes two people will date for years and then finally come to the conclusion that they don't belong together. When the relationship ends, there may be a period of depression.

And what happens when children are born with birth defects? When the body declines with age? When we lose abilities that once we had? Yes, we can look on these effects of sin, on these effects of living in a broken world, and we may mourn, and we me may fall into depression.

The effects of sin may cause depression. There's no direct guilt involved here. It's merely a symptom of living in a broken world.

Ah, but sometimes depression does come from direct sin. Sometimes it's caused by the sin of others.

A father abuses his child. She grows up hearing how worthless she is. How could she not suffer depression, having ingested that poison for years? Her hollow heart rings out, "Worthless!"

Another woman escapes an abusive husband. Now she suffers not only because of the messages she heard from him, but from those around her, too. After all, a good Christian woman wouldn't divorce her husband. He's such a nice man! And now all those messages get jumbled up in a wounded heart.

It's not just abuse, of course. A child leaves the faith. His parents reach out to him but are pushed back again and again. They know that because this child has left Jesus—this child whom they love, this child whom they raised—there is no hope for him when he dies. Yes, depression can well result from such a loss.

In the Psalms, David often cries out for help because his enemies line up against him. He is suffering because of the sin of others. Did he experience depression? I can't say that. I can say that the sin of others hurt him.

And sometimes our own sin causes depression.

Read Psalm 51. I'm not going to type it all out here. But go read it. David suffers, and it's his own fault. He's the one who sinned. He committed adultery. He murdered. He lied. And now all those sins come to light, and he cries out. Those sins haunted him for the rest of his life.

Maybe you committed a sin years ago, and it haunts you. The guilt has festered in your heart. It cries out, "You are worthless. How could you do such a thing? You pretend everything's fine, but if they knew the truth. If they knew!"

I understand. I struggle here. Have the sins of others hurt me? Certainly. Do the effects of sin cause me to mourn? Yes. And I do have a medical cause for my depression.

But here, I believe lies that make my depression so, so much worse.

We'll be talking about how to address depression later, so we're not going to get into how to fight against all these causes. Not here. Not yet.

But the short answer to all these causes, to all this world's sin, is the cross. Oh, Christian, look to the cross.

Jesus knew the effects of sin. He walked this broken world. He knew what it was to suffer from the sins of others. He experienced rejection and beatings. He knew. And though he never sinned, he knew your sins.

And he chose to die for you anyway.

You are loved, no matter the cause of your depression. You are forgiven, no matter your struggle.

And if you long for this message, we'll dig into it so, so much more later in this book.

Oftentimes, it's not a simple solution of saying "Well, clearly this is depression caused by a medical condition. Here's a pill; everything's better!" In my case, a combination of situational stresses, a guilty conscience, and a medical reality combined to create a severe depressive episode. Through counseling, I've learned how to handle those stresses far better. My depression is far more manageable now. However, I still have a lower amount of vitamin D in my blood, causing me to still slip into a depressive episode on occasion. Sometimes more often.

> *But the short answer to all these causes is the cross. Oh, Christian, look to the cross.*

So yes, recognize that there are many factors at play here. Trying to unravel them all yourself may not be wise. Restrain yourself from diagnosing depression in others or yourself. See a trained professional for yourself if you feel you might have depression. It is far more complex than simply telling someone "Cheer up! Jesus loves you!"

Chapter 8

Effects of Depression

DEPRESSION IS REAL. IT has a bunch of causes. And now we'll talk about the effects.

Which is really dumb.

I mean, really, if you've gotten this far in the book, you already know, don't you? Maybe you suffer from depression. You can shout "Look at my life! Look at the ruins around me. Look at my hollow heart. Once it was full of joy. Maybe. I think. I don't really remember. But I know it's not supposed to be like this—this empty hole in the middle of my chest. It only echoes my pain, my shame, my loneliness."

Maybe a friend or a family member suffers from depression. "I've seen them lay in bed, unable to move. Their eyes are dead. They want to play with the kids, but they just sit there. Nothing seems to bring them any happiness. They laugh, but you can tell it's not a real laugh. They're smiling, but there's nothing behind it."

And all of that is true . . . but it's good to list out how depression can affect a person. It's good to know that you're not alone in the struggle, that what you face is not only real, but it's also normal.

So what does depression look like? Feeling down, sad, detached, self-destructive, numb, experiencing an increase or loss of appetite, a loss of interest in sex—all of these things might hit the average person. The results can drag the average life into torture.

Many people focus on how depression can make someone feel sad. It's true. Feeling down, feeling blue, sobbing without any perceptible reason—all of these things happen.

In my life, it's less "sad" and more "empty." I don't feel happy. I don't feel down. I'm just . . . I just exist. I can't get excited about anything. My ability to be involved seems to vanish. I'll eat, but only because I know I should. I don't really taste the food. Loss in interest in sex? Yes, that is a very real thing.

In my life, one of the chief effects of depression is shame. The message I keep telling myself is "You're not good enough." I struggle with self-worth constantly, and it makes ministry difficult. I suspect every pastor who takes God's Word seriously feels unworthy to stand before the congregation and say "Thus says the Lord," at least occasionally. In my life, the feeling was nearly constant.

Another effect of my depression is an inability to deal with other people. I need to isolate myself constantly. I've become quite adept at canceling plans. If I do force myself to meet with people when I'm in a depressive episode, I can usually meet as needed. However, once I get home, I'll lie down in bed and not even be able to speak with my wife. As you might imagine, this isn't a positive addition to my ministry.

I don't know what's happened to you in your life. I don't know how depression has affected you personally or how you see it affect someone you love. But know this: You are not alone. Every person has been broken by sin. Depression is simply one more way our dying world infects us.

But Jesus has come for you. He didn't come just for people who don't have depression, for the happy-go-lucky types. He came for you. He loves you as his own. And your depression doesn't mean that God sees no use for you, either. If God can use someone like Elijah, he can use someone like you.

It's good to list out how depression can affect a person, to know that you're not alone in the struggle, that what you face is not only real, but it's also normal.

Chapter 9

Depression Is Not Something You Can Shake Yourself Out Of

YES, I'VE SAID IT before, but let me repeat it for the people in the back: depression is not something you can smile your way out of. Yes, through counseling a person can learn effective ways to work through the symptoms of depression. Yes, a person might be able to fake their way through. Yes, a person might even find coping mechanisms.

None of those things can cure depression, though. Depression might become harder for a season due to a number of factors, as it did in my life. Or it might become easier. Even if depression lets up, though, it will likely remain in the background.

That's what's happened in my life. I was first diagnosed with depression during a time of high stress. My counseling helped immensely. I'm now away from that stressful situation, and in general, I've got a good handle on my depression.

Except for some days.

Sometimes I can pinpoint what triggered the episode. When there are weeks that I push myself harder than usual, the second I relax, I usually slip into a funk. The week after Easter is often a dark time for me. Often enough, though, I can't predict when it'll hit. Maybe I'll be driving home after dropping the kids off at school. Maybe I'll be working on writing a book. It doesn't have any predictable pattern. And whether I can figure out the cause or it comes out of nowhere, I can't just shake myself out of it.

So sure. I "conquered my depression" by escaping that initial hard time. But now it continues to hollow out my heart and echo its lies.

One of the worst things a person can do is advise someone to just try and feel better. Just cheer up. One explanation from the internet reads:

I once tried to explain depression to someone as like if one day you gradually started to lose both your sense of taste and your ability to feel full. And you don't know why, but now everything you eat tastes like mashed potatoes and nothing you eat is satisfying. You keep eating because you must eat to live, but the effort that it takes to prepare food is taxing and there is no pay off. You just know it will taste like mashed potatoes. You just know you will still be hungry. So you stop bothering with seasonings. Then you stop bothering to use the ingredients you used to like. Then you start to wonder what the point of eating is because there is no payoff. You

> *Depression is real, it is lifelong, and it is not something you can shake yourself out of.*
>
> *If a person could escape depression that way, trust me, they would.*

still feel hungry and you're sick of the taste and you don't know if you will ever enjoy food again and you don't know why this is happening.

If someone comes up to you in this scenario and says, "Well have you tried spicing your food? Using different ingredients? Eating foods you used to love?" It isn't necessarily helpful because the reason you stopped doing all that in the first place is that everything . . . tasted . . . like . . . mashed . . . potatoes.[29]

Telling someone to just try to be happy does the opposite of help. Depression is real, it is lifelong, and it is not something you can shake yourself out of. If a person could escape depression that way, trust me, they would.

So don't feel bad if you can't shake yourself out of your depression. You might as well feel bad that you can't call down the rain.

Instead, rejoice that you are loved by your Lord, even in your depression.

---

29. Anonymous, "I once tried to explain depression," Facebook, accessed April 8, 2018.

Chapter 10

Depression Is Not a Sin

GOD DOES NOT SAY, "Be happy always! I say it again: Be happy!" In fact, Jesus promised the opposite: "I have told you these things, so that you may have peace in me. In this world you are going to have trouble. But be courageous! I have overcome the world."[30]

I trust that isn't a surprise to you. All of us have been around long enough to have seen the brokenness of this world in up close and personal ways. You've felt the tears fill your eyes. You've seen the blood well from the wound. You have scars on your arms and on your heart. You've seen Jesus's promise played out. You've seen trouble. I pray you have also experienced and shared the peace of knowing that Jesus has overcome the world.

Yet, far too often when I feel down, I'm given the well-intentioned advice "Cheer up!" As if our goal is simply to get someone to smile. Make no mistake, happiness is a blessing! But I wonder if in our hurry to cheer people up, we are unintentionally teaching that to be down is wrong. The Pixar movie *Inside Out* taught a valuable lesson our world needs to hear: Happiness is not always the best option. Sadness really has a place.

---

30. John 16:33

Depression is not a sin. Sorrow is not a transgression. Feeling down is not evil. Depression is an effect of sin. It is the result of living in a world broken away from God, so that even the chemicals in our own brains often conspire against us. All creation groans under the weight,[31] and our own brains are part of that creation. We are surrounded by the effects of sin. People sin against us. We live in the ruins of our own sin.

Jesus himself was familiar with sorrow.[32] And we know that there is no sin in Jesus. I don't think it's a leap outside of Scripture, then, to say that sorrow is not a sin.

Even our reactions to depression need not be sinful. Consider how Job spoke with God about the terrible things that had happened in his life. Yet we're told Job did not sin in his reaction.[33] Or consider David, crying out to God in the Psalms as we discussed earlier.

Again, depression is not a sin. It is an effect of sin.

However, depression can lead to sin. For some, it leads to a rejection of God's promises. A friend of mine who struggled with depression said he hated God. He knew Jesus had promised trouble, and he was tired of the trouble he had. He was convinced that only bad things would happen until he was brought to heaven, solely by grace. His depression led him to claim that God connived to make his life terrible.

You might point out that trusting that Jesus died for him and at the same time believing that God connived against him is hardly a logical position. You'd be right. But depression isn't always logical.

---

31. Romans 8:22 (NIV).
32. Isaiah 53:3
33. Job 1:22

46

Commenting on Psalm 74, Ingvar Floysvik writes:

The psalm ends as the main body began, with the enemies roaring. The tension is not resolved. The psalmist professes faith in God as the supreme unrivaled king of the universe and as the one who has entered into a relationship with Israel. The present reality bluntly contradicts this belief. The enemies have carried and still carry the day. The very existence of God's helpless people is in the balance.[34]

Floysvik later notes:

The questions do not look for an academic answer. They express bewilderment and protest . . . God is not supposed to be like this for he is the God of my salvation. He is characterized by steadfast love and faithfulness. He works wonders and acts of righteousness. Why does God not act toward me in conformity with the way he is?[35]

For others, depression leads to thinking less of God's creation. David cried out, "You wove me together in my mother's womb!"[36] A person with depression might

> *Depression is not a sin. It is an effect of sin. However, depression can lead to sin.*

say "I am nothing." Either that, or they may look at that verse and agree God gave them a great gift, but they've ruined it. This thinking leads even deeper into depression. "I am not worthy" is a refrain I'm very familiar with. And it doesn't lead to the awe of saying "And God loves *me*!" but rather, "God can't love me. And if he does, he's insane."

---

34. Ingvar Floysvik, *When God Becomes My Enemy* (Saint Louis, MO: Concordia Academic Press, 1997), 91.

35. Floysvik, *When God Becomes My Enemy*, 110.

36. Psalm 139:13

Rich Mullins sums up the thought well: "I grew up hearing everyone tell me 'God loves you'. I would say big deal, God loves everybody. That don't make me special! That just proves that God ain't got no taste."[37] In depression, the love of God initially hurts. The lies our hearts tell us lead us to say "He shouldn't!" and we rush from that love. "I am not good enough" repeats over and over again. "If you were good enough, she never would have left. If you were good enough, you'd have enough money. If you were good enough, you wouldn't still wrestle with your anger. If you were good enough, you wouldn't be tempted to visit that website again. If you were good enough..." And when that voice screams, "If you were good enough," hearing that God loves you feels like getting a consolation prize. Like pity. It only reminds you of your unworthiness. Depression has led to the sins of despising God's undeserved love and devaluing self.

And yet, that love is exactly what the person with depression needs. Rich Mullins finishes his statement by saying, "And, I don't think He does [have good taste]. Thank God! Because He takes the junk of our lives and makes the most beautiful art."[38] We'll address how to respond to depression in self and others in a more concrete way later, but the person with depression needs so, so much Gospel. We don't need tips and tricks. We don't need someone assuring us that it'll get better. We need Jesus. We need to see him on the cross. We need to see the objective truth of his love, that no matter what lies our hearts shout out, we are loved, just as we are, depression and all.

---

37. Rich Mullins, *Rich Mullins: Home* (Nashville, TN: VoxCorp, 1998). (I have not been able to find a recording of the live concert where he said this, but it can also be found in the book listed here.)
38. Rich Mullins, *Rich Mullins: Home.*

One picture that continues to break my stony heart goes like this: Jesus *knew* me. He knew the secrets. He knew those things I have never told anyone else. Those things that I know would destroy my ministry, my family, my life. Jesus knew all those things. He didn't gloss over them. He looked at them oh so very carefully. And then he said, "I choose to love you. I choose to die for you." For this reason, one of my favorite verses remains, "But God shows his own love for us in this: While we were still sinners, Christ died for us."[39] While I still believe the lies of my depression, Christ loves me. While I still tell God he is a liar, he loves me. While I think I am nothing, Jesus transforms me and makes me something. Here is grace that breaks my heart.

Yet, the depression that is not a sin may lead me to believe other lies, too. It might lead me to believe "Your internal hurt is better on the outside." I suspect that if you have never known someone who has intentionally hurt themselves, it is because they were afraid to tell you. But now you do know one: I was a cutter. I used a razor to intentionally hurt myself. Thankfully, that temptation is past in my life. I have not had a recurrence.

If this idea is foreign to you, praise God that you have never struggled with the thought. What happens is that the pain inside is so great, causing pain to the outside of your body actually lessens suffering. It focuses the pain into one spot on the body. Yes, you're right. It's not logical. Depression is not logical. When depression makes someone feel empty, hollow, the pain can "wake them up." It's a short-term solution that helps in no way.

---

39. Romans 5:8

Depression leads me to believe a lie: It is good to intentionally harm the body that God has given me. The same body God knit together in my mother's womb. The body that is fearfully and wonderfully made, that he designed just for me. Believing this destructive lie is indeed a sin. But it cannot be healed with more Law. You tell me that it's wrong and even stupid to hurt myself—you feed the lies. You're telling me again I'm not good enough. You're telling me that the lies I believe are true.

How do you overcome it?

Again, someone broken by depression needs love. Not shallow love. Not love that looks away. Not permissive love. Love that is not afraid to look at the wounds and say "I love you still. And what's more, Jesus loves you still." That person desperately needs to hear the Gospel.

Meanwhile, depression just keeps whispering lies. Depression might lead me to believe the lie "The light has ended. My life will never get better. It would be best for me and for those I love if I died." I am thankful that though I was a cutter, I never considered suicide.

I suspect you know someone who has at least attempted suicide. I do have good news: Just because someone has depression, it doesn't mean they're suicidal. Nearly 7% of the population in the US has depression.[40] "Only" about 0.5% of the population attempts suicide.[41] (It should be noted that numbers for teen suicide attempts are dramatically higher. In 2015, 8.6% of high schoolers self-reported a suicide attempt.[42])

---

40. "Facts and Statistics," Anxiety and Depression Association of America, accessed June 25, 2018, https://adaa.org/about-adaa/press-room/facts-statistics.
41. "Suicide Statistics," American Foundation for Suicide Prevention, accessed June 25, 2018, https://afsp.org/about-suicide/suicide-statistics/.
42. American Foundation for Suicide Prevention, "Suicide Statistics."

Suicide is a serious sin that claims God's gift of life is waste. It is murder. Depression may lead someone to believe the lie, though. And what then? How do you talk to someone that has attempted suicide? Again, this person needs Gospel so much. They need to know that Jesus loves them, broken as they are. They need to know that Jesus forgives even the sin of a suicide attempt.

You need to know that, too, if you've attempted suicide. Let me say it again: Jesus for-

> *Someone broken by depression needs love. Not shallow love. Not love that looks away. Not permissive love. Love that is not afraid to look at the wounds and say, "I love you still. . . .Jesus loves you still"*

gives you. He knows what you wanted to do. You might try to hide your attempt from others, but he is there with you.

And he loves you still.

You, even you, are forgiven. Jesus died for you. *You.*

We are not forgiven when we confess. Jesus died for our sins two thousand years ago. It is finished. Just because someone has committed suicide does not mean that person is sentenced to hell. Christians may be sinning when they die. Our hope for heaven is not based on our confession.[43] It is based on what Jesus has done in reality.

---

43. Romans 10:9 reminds us that confession is not something to be thrown away; I am focusing here on objective justification, the truth that Jesus has died for us. Period. He died for the sins of the whole world. He died for your sins.

Responding to Depression

Now what? Taking a closer look at how to encourage someone with depression, remind them (or yourself) of the truth, and see how even this can be a blessing.

Chapter 11

So . . . How Can I Help?

LET ME BEGIN BY saying what not to do. As one person responded to my informal survey of pastors who struggled with depression:

DO NOT SAY THAT I SIMPLY NEED STRONGER FAITH! I'm pretty emphatic on that point—sorry for the caps. When a person has clinical depression and is told that they need to have stronger faith or "simply trust God"— because of my depression, when that is said to me, I think, "So I don't have strong faith—what a horrible Christian I am." That simply serves to plunge me deeper into the black hole. Don't talk to me about faith, but simply point me to Jesus—who knows what I am going through. Point me to Jesus and give me His promises to which I can cling. Point me to Jesus and how God will take even this and work it for His glory and my good. . . . When I was in [Seminary], I was told to simply snap out of it and have faith. That did not work so well (sarcastically said).[44]

Let me say it, yes, again: Don't tell people to cheer up. Don't tell a depressed person he shouldn't have depression. Doing so is preaching a form of the theology of glory.

We already talked about this a little bit, but a reminder is good. The

---

44. Italiano, "Depression in the Ministry Survey," emphasis in original.

theology of glory says that the life of a Christian should be easy. As long as a Christian believes, as long as a Christian tries hard, everything should work out fine.

The theology of glory is heresy. Sometimes when we read that word, we think that's a thing for theological bigwigs in seminaries to worry about. It's arguing about tiny little things that have nothing to do with real life.

Some heresies might be like that, but not this one. This one will eat you whole if you believe it.

If the theology of glory is real, then you should be able to believe your way out of any problem. You don't have enough money? Just believe harder. You've got cancer? You need to have more faith. Your mother disowned you? Well, if you were a good Christian, that wouldn't happen.

> *But if it's all about having enough faith, then the pressure's all on you to fix it. . . . The weight on your soul gets to be too much, and your hollow heart begins to crack.*

I hope you know that in all those cases, every single one of them, all this theology does is drive someone into the dirt.

Rather, listen to the truth. You don't have enough money? Neither did Jesus. At one point he commented that he had no place to lay his head.[45] Jesus had perfect faith. If faith was all it took to have an easy life, he should have had the easiest.

---

45. Matthew 8:20

Greater faith won't heal cancer, either. God might bless you with healing. He might use that cancer to bring you home. Job was afflicted with terrible sickness, and yet he didn't lack faith.[46]

Your mother disowned you? Jesus said that those who are faithful to him will be disowned.[47]

With each of these, I'm not saying suffering guarantees you've got great faith. We live in a broken world, and people suffer. You don't have to be Christian to suffer. But faith does not protect you from suffering, either. At the beginning of time, God pronounced a curse on the world as a result of sin.[48] We all labor under that curse, and we won't be freed until we see Jesus face-to-face.

What that means for you is that you can accept suffering as a part of this broken world, but you know this world is not the end of the story.

But if you believe the theology of glory, then every time you suffer, it's your fault. Period. If you just believed harder, well, you wouldn't have that problem.

Maybe you've felt that pressure. Particularly with mental illness, well-meaning Christians try to help by encouraging us to "Just believe. Just have more faith. It's all in your head."

Of course it's all in your head. Where else would mental illness be?

But if it's all about having enough faith, then the pressure's all on you to fix it. Just do a little more. Trust a little more. Come on. You can do it. Everyone else seems fine. Why can't you be fine?

---

46. Job 1
47. Luke 12:53
48. Genesis 3:14–19

And every day, the strain grows. Every day, the pressure increases. Every day, you try to hold it together. You try to fake it so no one looks down on you. But the weight on your soul gets to be too much, and your hollow heart begins to crack.

Oh, do not believe this theology of glory. Don't do it! It will destroy you.

And then you get the other side of the coin of the theology of glory. If your life is put together, it's because you believe enough. Did you conquer depression? Good job! You know who gets the credit? All you! After all, you had the faith to destroy it! Why can't everyone else be like you?

Do you hear the utter arrogance there? God doesn't get the credit. You do.

It's not a good look.

Christian, brother, sister, whoever you are who reads these words now, do not fall for that terrible heresy that will either plunge you into despair or to boost you to arrogance. Either direction leads to destruction.

> *When I am hurting deeply . . . I need more than the math of things. I need to know that my Father feels pain intensely as I do. . . that he sees me and that he cares.*

So if you have a friend who struggles with depression, run from the theology of glory. "If you believe, your life will be better" will only damage the person you wish to help.

If you have done that to someone, a friend, a family member, let me urge you: repent. If it was done in ignorance, so be it. Repent. And know this: The same Jesus that died for the person with depression died for you, too. Jesus took care to not put out any smoldering wick.[49]

Have you ever blown out a candle? The wick will often glow red for just a moment afterward. It would be so, so easy to snuff that out. All you have to do is walk away, and the heat will dissipate.

But Jesus looks at those of us who have so little faith, who hurt so much. He doesn't walk away. He doesn't wait for us to die. He doesn't say to the flame, "Well, if you tried hard enough, you could light yourself up again!" Instead, he nurtures that flame. He blows on it. He reignites it. He cares about those whose fire is almost out. And that's what he does for the Christian who struggles with depression.

Perhaps in carelessness, callousness, or ignorance, you snuffed out a wick. Be comforted that you do not wear your own righteousness. A righteousness apart from following the Law has been made known.[50] You now wear Jesus's record. You are forgiven. You are free of the sins of your past, and all the sins of your future, too. When Jesus looks at you, he doesn't see the times you damaged someone with the theology of glory. He doesn't see the times you snuffed out someone's hope. He sees someone who loves perfectly.

It may seem odd, but theological explanations probably aren't what's needed for the person with depression, either. Yes, avoid heresy, please! But the person you're helping may know all the theories and key verses. They may have used them on themselves, beating themselves up for not trusting Jesus's promises enough.

---

49. Matthew 12:20
50. Romans 3:21

When I am hurting deeply, formal theology explanations of suffering never seem to calm my restless soul because long-term pain isn't something that logic alone can fix. If the Lord is going to allow the world to be this brutal, I need more than the math of things. I need to know that my Father feels pain intensely as I do and that his love for me will prove stronger than any single moment of weakness that suffering evokes. I need to be free to cry out to him, knowing that he sees me and that he cares.[51]

And now I'm going to address those of you who struggle with depression. Perhaps you don't. If you don't struggle with depression, first, praise God. Second, look on this as an example of how to address someone who battles depression.

---

51. Reynolds, *Courage, Dear Heart*, 57.

Chapter 12

You Are Loved

I DON'T KNOW THE exact variation of the lies your depression whispers to you. But I know how convincing those lies can be. I know it seems your heart is the one telling you these things, and everything in our culture tells you to trust your heart.

Your heart lies.[52] Do not trust it. Even now. Especially now.

Jesus knows your depression. He knows the exact form it takes for you. He knows the lies. And he's not ashamed of you. He knows what you've kept secret. He knows what I don't know. And he's not ashamed of you. He's not ashamed to call you "brother."[53] "We forgot then and we forget now that Jesus is for losers and for losers only."[54] He is for you.

He takes your shame and he looks at it. I don't know what that shame is, but Jesus does. And if that shame is sin, he condemns it. He sees it for the darkness it is. He sees it for the filth it is. But your secrets and your depression and your guilt will not pay for your sin. No matter how bad you feel, you cannot remove it.

---

52. Jeremiah 17:9
53. Hebrews 2:11
54. Jared C. Wilson, *The Pastor's Justification* (Wheaton, IL: Crossway, 2013), 78.

But Jesus did. Your weakness, your shame, your sin, all of it. He chose to take it from you.

I know you know this already. But it is so, so easy to believe the lie that Jesus died for *them*, but not for *me*. Or that he only died for me because I'm part of the package of "everyone." And so you try to live up to Jesus, to not be so bad.

You don't need more Law. You need more Gospel.

You, even you, are loved.

Before [my adopted son], I didn't understand what fierce love God holds for those he has adopted into his family. I didn't realize that when he pursues us, he knows all our damage and our defects—and he knows exactly where we rank on every system humans use to determine our value. He stares straight into all of the world's opinions of us and yet proclaims that we are the *wanted ones*. No matter how anybody has let us down, hurt us, forgotten us, we are still longed for and beloved children.[55]

But my love for him is so weak. And it is.

Though Israel had played the prostitute whoring after false gods, the prophets cry the constancy of God in the face of human infidelity: "Israel, don't ever be so foolish as to measure my love for you in terms of your love for me! Don't ever compare your thin, pallid, wavering, and moody love with my love, for I am God, not man."[56]

Depression does not love you. It does not hold you close and whisper sweet nothings to you. It longs to enslave you. Its desire is to destroy

---

55. Reynolds, *Courage, Dear Heart,* 39, emphasis in original.
56. Brennan Manning, *The Ragamuffin Gospel* (Sisters, OR: Multnomah Publishers, 2000), 100.

you. It tells you that you are not wanted. It screams that you are not enough. It whispers that if you were known, you would be rejected forever. Your hollow heart echoes those lies.

But depression does not have you. Jesus has purchased and won you. You are not his consolation prize. You aren't one of those miscellaneous "and you also won . . . !" things that come at the end of a game show.

Jesus paid for you, not with gold or silver, but with his holy precious blood and his innocent suffering and death.[57]

You.

Depression does not have you. You have depression. Jesus has you.

I've used this trick for years, and I'd like to recommend it to you now: Pretty much anytime the Bible says "the world" or "us" in some form, you can put "me" or "mine" in its place. Yes, Jesus came for all people, and we must not forget that. Let's not slip into some arrogant idiocy that says that Jesus came for me and only me.

But for you who struggle with depression, who claim to be unloved, who feel so unloved, use this trick.

"For God so loved the world that he gave his only-begotten Son, that whoever believes in him shall not perish, but have eternal life."[58]

Yes. God loved the entire world. That person over there. And that guy walking by. Oh, and don't forget her!

You know who else he loved?

"For God so loved *you* that he gave his only-begotten Son."

---

57. Martin Luther and David P. Kuske, "Explanation to the Second Article," in *Luther's Catechism* (Milwaukee, WI: Northwestern Publishing House, 1989), 156.
58. John 3:16

If you were the only sinner in the world, Jesus still would have come for you. You are loved that much, dear one. I know it can hurt to hear that. I know the lies shout louder to drown out the sound of his love.

So simply know this: Jesus embraces you. He washes you clean. He claims you as his brother, his sister.

You are his own.

> *Your depression tells you that you are not loved.*
> *It screams that you are not enough.*
> *Your hollow heart echoes those lies . . .*
> *But depression does not have you.*
>
> *You have depression. Jesus has you.*

Chapter 13

You Are Not Alone

DO YOU RECALL THE lists of prophets who may have suffered depression? Depression isolates. It drives us to lonely places. Even when surrounded by friends, we feel alone. Even when we *know* others love us, we feel unworthy. Our hollow hearts imprison us in a dark and lonely cell.

Oh, but you are not alone.

Here I am. I have depression. You do not walk this road alone. You are not the only one who knows the joy of the Lord while toiling under the impossible burden of a hollow heart. And you and I aren't freaks for having depression.

I know it feels like you need to keep it secret. You do need to exercise wisdom when deciding with whom to share your depression. We'll talk about that soon. But you don't need to keep it hidden because you fear you are alone. You are not.

"But I know better." I know you do. I do, too. Every time I slip into one of my episodes, I beat myself up. Haven't I learned the lesson already? Don't I already know that my worth is not in me but in the robes of righteousness my Savior won for me? Even in this, you're not alone. And just as we constantly need to hear the Gospel, so often we need to be reminded of other things we know. You are not alone.

But this by itself isn't much comfort. It just means we're messed up together, doesn't it?

Look to your Savior. Do you see him weep?[59] Do you hear him as he cries out, in a situation where the brokenness of this world strikes at his heart? He sobs because the effects of sin have taken his dear friend Lazarus. His friend is dead. Jesus has already said he will raise Lazarus from the dead. It's not something he's unsure of. He knows that his friend will walk from the grave in just a few minutes! But even then, he still bawls. Your Savior knows what it is to weep.

> *You do not walk this road alone. Jesus has walked this way before. Even now, he is walking with you.*

I know you are tempted to despair. I know that temptation to walk away can be so strong. But Jesus faced that temptation. He knows what it is. Every temptation you've faced, he has, too. And he has overcome.[60] He didn't overcome to give you an example. He did it to give you the victory he won. Your depression has already been defeated by your Savior. "On the cross, He carried not only our transgressions and our iniquity, but 'our infirmities' and 'our sorrows.' "[61]

He has already walked through the valley of the shadow of death. You have experienced what it is to have the walls cut off the sun. You have lost sight of the sky. The heavens have been far, far beyond your grasp.

---

59. John 11:35

60. Hebrews 4:15

61. Gene Edward Veith Jr., *The Spirituality of the Cross* (St. Louis, MO: Concordia Publishing House, 1999), 59.

But Jesus has walked this way before. He has passed through and seen the bright sunlight on the other side. He is guiding you even now. Even now, he is walking with you. And when your heart lies to you, when it says that you are forgotten, remind it of this truth: Your Savior knows your depression, loves you still, and stands with you. You are never alone.

Chapter 14

You Are Not What You Do

WHO YOU ARE DOES not depend on what you do. I don't know about you, but I'm pretty busy. I don't get everything done every day. I fail more often than I like admitting (particularly before my church council). I don't make as many evangelism visits as I want. I don't follow up as well as I think I should. I don't spend as much time preparing sermons as I feel I should.

Your list probably has different items on it, but let's face it: you probably don't accomplish what you're convinced should be done. Should you be doing more at work? Sure, maybe not what your boss thinks you should be doing. But should you be excelling? Should you have a better position, more pay, more respect? Should you be keeping your house in better order? Look at that pile of dishes. The living room is filthy. How long has it been since you changed your bedsheets? Oh, and what about yourself? Are you improving yourself? Are you growing new skills? Are you learning? How's your health? Are you exercising enough? Why haven't you been out on a date in forever?

Feel the pressure growing?

It's so, so easy to look at all the things you've failed to do. Maybe it's a list that others have given you. Maybe it's one you've formed yourself. However you got the list of things you "have to do," it is long, it is daunting, and it is incomplete. Your hollow heart echoes the cries for you to do more, get more done, keep going, don't stop!

Jesus does not demand that we accomplish all these tasks. Jesus does not command me to carry the congregation on my back. He doesn't command you to complete all your tasks. It is not about what you do.

It is about what your Shepherd has done. Remember who you are and who your Savior is.

Your Shepherd cares for *you*. Your Shepherd laid down his life for you, only to take it up again. And he doesn't do that to guilt you. I know that your depression might make you feel worse when I say that. But did you know? "For the joy set before him."[62] Jesus didn't look at you and sigh, "Fine, you get thrown in, too." No. For the joy of rescuing *you,* his sheep, he has endured the cross, scorning its shame.

He didn't choose you because of everything you could do. He chose you because he loved you. And when he chose you, when he adopted you, when he made you his own, he changed who you are. "So then, if anyone is in Christ, he is a new creation. The old has passed away. The new has come!"[63]

You are not what you do. You are God's chosen, beloved child.

You are not your failures. You are Jesus's chosen brother, sister.

You are not "not good enough." You are made perfect in Jesus.

---

62. Hebrews 12:2 (NIV).
63. 2 Corinthians 5:17

This is who you are. You are not failure. Not an incomplete list. Not just a string of "should"s. None of these things define you.

You are God's child.

Do not forget who you are. If you are what you do, you will never be good enough. You'll only see your failures. If you are what you should do, you will "should" yourself into despair. These things are not your identity. Your identity is one that cannot be taken from you, because it's not based on what you do. It's based on what Jesus has done. Who you are does not depend on what you do.

And this is all true no matter your role.

Your hollow heart echoes the cries for you to do more, get more done, keep going, don't stop! But it is not about what you do. It is about what your Shepherd has done.

Are you a mother? Oh, you feel the guilt that comes with that role, don't you? Have you loved your child enough? Did you breast feed your child? Did you bottle feed? You monster! (I'm not sure which one is the monster here . . . either way depending who you listen to.) Do you feed your children healthy foods? Do you squash them by not allowing them to have sugar? Are the kids too busy? Not involved enough? Oh, there is so much pressure for the mother. And if your identity is "mother," you'll never find peace.

But your identity is not "mother." That describes a role you hold for now. It is a good role, but it is not who you are. Your identity is "Daughter of the Most High." That is who you really are. And if that is who you are, even when you fail in your role, your identity remains. You are loved, even when you fail. You are valued. You are God's daughter.

Are you a hard worker? What happens when you can't work hard anymore? Is your health failing? Are you too busy in another role, like father or mother? Did something change at work and you simply don't know how to do that work anymore? And now your entire self-concept is falling apart. Everything you thought you were is a lie.

Except it is not a lie. You are not "hard worker." You are "Child of the Most High." You may have been blessed with the ability to work hard and work well, but those things are roles you hold for a little bit. You will be a child of the Most High for eternity. He didn't pick you because of your hard work. He picked you because he loves you. Jesus says, "You did not choose me, but I chose you and appointed you to go and bear fruit, fruit that will endure, so that the Father will give you whatever you ask in my name."[64] Yes, your hard work is a consequence of who you are. But that is not who you are.

You may believe that you are your depression. It's so easy to define ourselves by what is wrong with us. It's so, so easy to look in the mirror and see only our brokenness.

Oh, dear one, you are not your depression. Just as depression does not own you, it also does not define you.

When Jesus sees you, he does not see that darkness that threatens to consume you. Do you know what he sees?

He sees *you*.

---

64. John 15:16

He sees his brother, his sister. He sees a child of his Father. He sees someone he has chosen to save. He comes and wraps his arms around you. He is not afraid of you getting him dirty. After all, he bled for you. He does not fear your filth. He does not flinch at the lies you've believed. He comes to tell you the Truth.

He is the Resurrection and the Life. He has come to give you himself. He holds nothing back.

You are not your depression. Your depression describes a part of your life. For now. It will not remain. Who you are will remain into eternity.

Who are you?

You are a child of God.

Chapter 15

Your Heart Lies

"FOLLOW YOUR HEART."

It sounds so good, doesn't it? "Chase your dreams. Reach out, and make your imagination reality."

In some cases, it's good advice. You have the talents to be a doctor? You want to use those gifts to bless others around you? Go. Do the work. Chase that dream, and use that role of doctor to serve the world.

But what happens when your heart is set on something that lies outside your gifts? You want to be a doctor, but God hasn't given you those skills. You chase your dreams . . . but all comes to ruin.

What happens when your heart leads you to love someone that you can never have? What happens when your heart leads you to love someone you *should* never have? Perhaps you're married, but now your heart urges you to pursue another. Maybe you desperately want to form a relationship with someone who is not interested or someone who is already committed to another.

What happens when your hollow heart echoes out despair? What happens when your heart whispers that you're worthless? What happens when your heart only speaks shame?

I've said it before, and I'll say it again: Your heart lies. It twists truths to grind you down so you cannot see how loved you are and how Jesus has fought your battle for you.

And I know in that moment of distress, you may know the truth, but at that moment it is like knowing random facts about ocelots. Sure, it may be true, but it doesn't affect you. What your experience says at that moment and what you know God's Word has told you are in complete conflict. In that hour of darkness, your heart wants to drag you down with a millstone and drown you in despair.

In that hour when you cannot fight your heart anymore, when its lies have led you to the edge, know this:

> *Your heart lies.*
> *The next time your heart*
> *condemns you, remember:*
> *Jesus is bigger than your heart.*

You cannot hold on to God. He holds on to you.

You are not strong enough. You do not have to be strong enough. You are not less because you are not strong enough.

The LORD is your strength.[65] He is the one who has become your salvation. It is his responsibility to rescue you. He is the Redeemer—not you. Be weak. Be weak in the Lord. Rest.

Be still. Know that he is God.[66]

I know your heart lies. It tells you to hate yourself. It tells you that you are not good enough.

---

65. Exodus 15:2, Psalm 28:7, Psalm 118:14, Isaiah 12:2, Habakkuk 3:19
66. Psalm 46:10

And how does it end when the war that you're in
is just you against you against you?
You've got to learn to love, learn to love,
learn to love your enemies, too.[67]

No, I'm not encouraging you to become selfish and ignore the needs of others. And yes, I know that you have sinned in thought, word, and deed. No, I don't know all your sins. But I know you have reason to hate yourself.

How difficult it is to be honest, to accept that I am unacceptable, to renounce self-justification, to give up the pretense that my prayers, my spiritual insight, tithing, and successes . . . have made me pleasing to God! No antecedent beauty enamors me in His eyes. I am lovable only because He loves me.[68]

I also know that Jesus has redeemed you, a lost and condemned sinner, purchased and won you, not with silver or gold, but with his holy, precious blood and his innocent suffering and death.[69] *You.* This is a truth bigger than your heart. And the next time your heart condemns you, remember: Jesus is bigger than your heart.[70]

Your heart lies. That's why you need to be in God's Word. Scripture does not lie to you. When all is darkness, stand in the Light.

It will tell you that your sins are real, but that forgiveness is just as real. And it will help with the other lies you may believe. It will convict you of sin and point you to Jesus as the solution to that sin.

---

67. Andrew Peterson, "Be Kind to Yourself," track 8 on *The Burning Edge of Dawn,* Centricity Music, 2015, MP3.
68. Manning, *The Ragamuffin Gospel,* 83.
69. Luther and Kuske, "Explanation to the Second Article," 156.
70. 1 John 3:20

It will tell you that you are loved. That even while you were filthy, the Father welcomed you home with open arms, celebrating.

Consider the story that Jesus tells in Luke 15. Some people call it the Parable of the Prodigal Son:

A father had two boys. The younger one said to his dad, "I can't wait for you to die. Give me what'll be mine after you, you know, keel over."

And dad did it!

Shortly after, the son left home. The Bible says he spent the money in "wild living." And then a famine hit. His friends dried up as quickly as the fields. He ended up working on a pig farm to survive.

I've worked on a pig farm. The job interview was simple: Walk through the barn. If you can make it through without vomiting, you're hired. And yes, I'm serious. That was the actual job interview. The smell is so overpowering and so awful, if you can survive it, you're in for as long as you want.

The thing they don't tell you is that the smell gets into the pores of your skin. Even after you shower, even after you scrub and scrub with soap, the scent lingers. When you hug someone, they know where you work. If you stay in the profession long enough, people will be able to tell when you enter the room by smell alone.

And so the boy in Jesus's story worked on the pig farm. We don't know how long he worked there. But he finally realized, "This is dumb. My dad has employees who eat better than I do. I'll go back. I'll admit that I sinned against him. I sinned against heaven! I'll ask to just work for him. That's all. I'll work, and he'll pay me, and it'll be fine."

So the boy set out to go home. As he did, he passed by some fields that belonged to his dad. He didn't recognize any of the workers, though.

"Oh, yeah. Dad sold the fields off to give me my share. I hope he's not still angry."

Then he finally got to fields where he recognized the workers . . . but there weren't nearly as many cattle in the fields as there used to be.

"Oh, yeah. Dad sold half the herds for me. Do you think . . . Is it possible he's still angry?"

And then he came over a rise and looked down on the home he grew up in. It still stood. And there on the path to the house, a man sprinted toward him.

His father.

Of course he was still angry. Of course he was furious. Why wouldn't he be? Why would he ever let his son back, even as a worker?

So the boy called out, "Dad! I'm sorry! I've sinned against heaven! I've sinned against you!"

And before he could say any more, his breath was squeezed out of him as his father embraced him in the fiercest bear hug you've ever seen. The boy reeked. The stench of pig clung to him.

His dad didn't care.

He had taken half of everything his dad owned. His dad should have been so, so angry.

His dad didn't care.

A servant rushed up behind dad. He heaved for breath. "Sir?"

Dad turned around. "Go put the steaks on the grill! Get out the wine—the good stuff! Look! Here's my son!"

And the father looked at his son. He breathed in the stench. He saw the dirty clothes. "My son! Look! He was lost, and he's found! He was dead, and he's alive!"

Do you hear these words? That joy?

It doesn't matter what stench your heart unburies. It doesn't matter what lies it speaks. This is what the Father speaks to you. In all your stench, in all your filth, the Father looks at you and declares, "You were lost, and I've found you! You were dead in your sins, and now look! I've made you alive!"

This is the truth. No matter how loudly your heart shouts, it lies. It cannot change the way the Father feels about you.

Your heart lies.

> *No matter how loudly your heart shouts, it lies. It cannot change the way the Father feels about you.*

I know how hard it is to disbelieve lies whispered from within, even when you know better. On those days you cannot fight . . . rest. Just rest. God has you. His nail-scarred hands will not let you go.[71] Go back. See his promises to *you*. See how he's wild about you and was willing to pay any price for you. You are of great enough worth to God that he chose to rescue you. And not only that, but you can rest secure in him.

Your heart lies.

Your Savior is the Truth.

Trust him more than you would your heart.

---

71. John 6:39

Chapter 16

Get Help

I UNDERSTAND.

You're not supposed to need this kind of help. You're supposed to have your life together. You're supposed to be good enough to stand on your own two feet. If you're falling apart, you should be able to fake it well enough, at the least.

Let's be honest, shall we? You are just as broken as the people around you. If the people around you need help, you need it, too. And even if they didn't, even if their lives were as put together as they seem, it wouldn't change the fact that you need help.

You know the truth. Satan attacks you powerfully, and if he can use depression to drive you from Christ, to make you think you need to carry this burden, to tear down your life and the lives of those who love you, don't you think he's going to do it? If he can isolate you, he can destroy you so much more easily. And if you're convinced you shouldn't ask for help, you are isolated, whether you want to admit it or not. You are not immune to the pressures of mental illness. Unless you're more stoic than Jesus, you face the possibility of emotional hardship.

If you fell and broke a bone, you would feel no shame going to a doctor to get the necessary medical aid. You certainly wouldn't feel the need to hide it from those around you! If you battle depression, get help. Yes, you may need to exercise wisdom in who to share your need with, and we'll address that a little later. But still: Get help.

This may be the most difficult step in dealing with depression. It means admitting we can't do it on our own. And as much as we say we depend on Christ, don't we so often get mini-Messiah complexes? We think we need to save ourselves.

Oh, but that's not true. Your heart is lying to you.

We think we must be strong.

We are wrong.

Honesty brings an end to pretense through a candid acknowledgement of our fragile humanity. It is always unpleasant, and usually painful, and that is why I am not very good at it. But to stand in the truth before God and one another has a unique reward. It is the reward which a sense of reality always brings. I know something extremely precious. I am in touch with myself as I am. My tendency to play the pseudo-messiah is torpedoed.[72]

> *If you fell and broke a bone,*
> *you would feel no shame going to a*
> *doctor to get the necessary medical aid.*
> *You certainly wouldn't feel the need to*
> *hide it from those around you!*
> *If you battle depression, get help.*

---

72. Manning, *The Ragamuffin Gospel*, 138

Maybe you've reached the point when you're willing to admit to yourself that you need help. Good. But the next step is even harder. You need to live in community, being transparent with those closest to you. To receive help, you need to admit to those around you that you need it.

I have found one of the best ways to get help is to simply have a brother or sister (or more than one!) with whom I can speak candidly. If you're having a bad day, have someone that you can call up. I remember at a previous congregation calling a fellow pastor up and saying "Today's a good day for a beer. Want to grab one with me?" We went out, grabbed some drinks, and talked. And it's what I needed. Simply having a place to lay down all the masks of "I'm okay" and let out what's really going on inside can relieve so much pressure.

But if you've got depression and you're an introvert like I am, calling up a friend probably doesn't sound attractive at all. Talking to someone face-to-face isn't always the best thing, nor is it always practical. Thankfully, God has placed us at a time in history where we don't need to talk on the phone nor gallop on horseback to be able to let off steam to one another. I often use the chat feature on Facebook when I'm feeling down; it doesn't trip off my "introvert sensors" but can still give very real support. That won't work for everyone, but it may be worth a try.

No matter how you connect with this trusted friend, let me urge you: be honest with him or her. It shouldn't be a whining fest. Rather, be open about your struggles. Let out the lies you've been struggling with.

Obviously this is not the same as counseling, professional or otherwise. Don't regard this companionship as something that will fix you. Oftentimes counseling is needed; we'll get to that.

If you're a friend who someone is sharing with, let me urge you: Don't seek to correct. God didn't correct Elijah immediately.[73] Don't give some pithy advice. Jesus didn't tell Martha to cheer up.[74] Instead, listen. Then listen some more. After that, keep listening. And when your friend has spoken what he or she needs to speak, *then* remind them of what they already know. Do it gently. If your friend has confessed a sin, by all means, show them what Jesus has done for them. Speak forgiveness to them. If you see a sin that needs to be confessed after all that, certainly address it, but again, gently. Be a friend, because that's what's needed at that moment.

I hope you have a friend like that. It's so, so hard to open up like that. This kind of transparency is difficult in our world, when we often have shallow relationships which depend on us being okay, being happy, relaxed, fun to be around. Opening up is a risk.

However, the Bible instructs us to live in community with one another.[75] If you don't know who to open up to, speak to your pastor. He may have some suggestions for you. If your congregation has small groups, take advantage of that opportunity. They often serve as safe places to receive support. If you are mourning, mourn with others. Allow them to mourn with you.[76]

But I hope, if you have depression, you also receive some professional help. I received formal counseling from a brother pastor for two or three

---

73. 1 Kings 19
74. John 11
75. 1 Corinthians 13
76. Romans 12:15

months. It wasn't long, but this counseling helped me identify the lies my heart spoke and helped me learn how to use God's Word against those particular lies.

If you go to a pastor for this formal counseling, please look for someone who has had some sort of specialized training. The man I saw had received training and had experience. He directed me to God's Word often, reminding me of the sure promises of Jesus.

Of course, you may want or need to speak to a trained therapist. I didn't need that in my situation, but at some point I may. You may be resistant to do so. But just as we're not ashamed if we need to take the car to a specialist or call in a plumber because something is blocked beyond our ability to unclog, we should not be ashamed to ask for help if our depression has grown to be too much. Our world is broken. We are broken. And we cannot fix ourselves. There is no shame in seeking help.

> *This kind of transparency is difficult in our world. Opening up is a risk.*

Sometimes one of the fears that keeps us from seeing a professional therapist is the possibility of medication. Depression medication can be terrifying. I've seen those medications backfire for friends; they can take away our passion, cause deeper depression, spark a more fiery temper, or have no effect at all. It can take weeks or months to discover if a medication is effective. If it is not effective, it can take just as long to wean off.

Should a Christian take antidepressants?

Let me ask this a different way: should a Christian with a medical problem make use of medication?

Now allow me some sarcasm: dur.

God has granted us the blessings of doctors and scientists who have been able to make medications and apply them well. I would urge caution and education. Not every medication is right for every individual, and good timing might help the process.

Pray for wisdom and investigate the possible side effects, along with the timeline required to determine effectiveness. Research the side effects for going off the medication. When I was first diagnosed with depression, I visited a psychiatrist who gave me two prescriptions. "Investigate these. You're borderline; you don't *need* these, but they may help you. If you want, try one of these. If not, don't." Both medications had a 30% chance of increased aggression, and I chose not to make use of either. I was in a situation with high stress, and increased aggression would not have helped! However, I was put on a vitamin D supplement I still take every day.

Since that time, my depression has grown worse, but I am also no longer in that time of high stress. I had to reevaluate. I now take two medications beyond vitamin D. These help stabilize me. I'm using a medical response to a medical problem, even as I also use God's Word to combat the lies my heart tells me.

Talk to your counselors. Get an opinion outside yourself. If you're blessed with a spouse, ask them for their opinion. Your spouse may tell you "Dear, get the meds." Do some research online. And pray. Keep praying.

It's outside the scope of this book to advise on all the many medications out there. But know that medications are not your enemy.

Chapter 17

Take Care of Yourself

ARE YOU THE KIND of person who sees everything that has to be done and then ignores your own needs? God gave the fifth commandment, "You shall not murder," for your own body, too. He wants us to take care of our bodies. Take care of this gift God's given to you.

That means you need to take time to rest. It's true we're all different and require different amounts of rest. One person might make do with a couple weeks off every summer; another needs a full weekend every week. Let's prevent ourselves from looking down on others if their rest habits are different from ours, but encourage one another toward faithfulness in taking care of these bodies.

You are not a just soul. God created you, body and soul, knit together in the most marvelous ways. That means your body matters. More than one person in my informal survey mentioned how exercising and eating right affected the body.[77] (I still have work to do on that one myself.) Do know that the body affects the mind. Eating well will help you regulate your depression. Exercising keeps both body and mind healthy. You

---

77. Italiano, "Depression in the Ministry Survey."

might play a sport, walk the dog, or lift weights. These are all great, and I encourage you to find out what works for you.

Tied to both making sure you get time off and eating and exercising well, you need to get enough sleep. The body functions better when rested. Your depression may decrease if you're getting enough shut-eye. Yes, I know there's so much more going on. Yes, I know your list of to-dos is massive. Trust me, I know!

> *The body affects the mind. Care for both.*

Does so much depend on *you*? Or have you picked up a burden designed to be shared, or even a burden that Jesus himself says he will carry?

Before Jesus came, God commanded that every seventh day be a day of rest. The Sabbath was a chance to rest both body and soul. People gathered to worship and then to relax together. God cared enough for the people to even command that they rest.

We are no longer under those Old Testament laws. God no longer commands that we rest every seventh day. Jesus is our great Sabbath rest.[78] God still cares about your body, though. Take the time to rest, knowing that he watches over you. The same God who died for you is the one who watches over you know.

In fact, he will watch over you both while you are awake and while you sleep. Yes, faithful servant, God uses you in his kingdom in marvelous ways. Yes, you are asked to be faithful. That faithfulness includes finding the time to sleep. Rest, and rest well. Take care of your body so you can be equipped to serve. Be still and know that he is God.[79]

---

78. Hebrews 4:1–14
79. Psalm 46:10

Chapter 18

But Who Do I Tell?

THE NEXT QUESTION IS how does this work day-to-day? If you are wounded and seeking help, if you will not hide it behind a mask of "It's all right," others will see the real you. And what then? How transparent should you be?

There is a great temptation to keep this struggle private. There are good reasons to be careful about sharing weakness, of course: It could be used as ammunition against you if someone doesn't like what you're saying. "You're only angry because you're struggling with depression. You're just trying to drag me down. Clearly you have a mental illness, so why should I trust what you have to say?" It could cause the end of relationships. "You're never happy like you used to be." Others might lower their opinion of you. "I thought you had it together. I guess I was wrong."

Sinning Christians and hypocrites have been leveling such assertions since the beginning of the Christian church. Members and outsiders in both the Galatian[80] church and Corinthian[81] church complained about Paul. And Paul is quite open with his weaknesses. "You know that, because of a weakness of the flesh, I preached the gospel to you the first time.

---

80. Thus Paul's defense in Galatians 1 and 2
81. Thus Paul's defense in 1 Corinthians 9

And you did not despise or disdain the test my flesh gave you. Instead, you welcomed me as an angel of God, as Christ Jesus."[82] This was no one-on-one conversation Paul was having; he placed it in a letter to be read publicly.

How many examples of possible depression did we see in God's leaders? And how many of them kept their struggles secret?

I know the fear you may feel in sharing your weakness. No one likes sharing their weaknesses. None of us like admitting how much we need Jesus in a real way—and not "simply" in some shallow or generic way, not in some socially acceptable way—but in a clinging to him with your fingernails because you need him that much and that badly way.

But there are great benefits in sharing.

I firmly believe that wise sharing of your weakness can give glory to Jesus.

Let me underline: Do be wise in how you share and how much you share. Not everyone needs to know every sordid detail of your struggles. Certainly, you do not want to be an offense. You don't want your weakness to be an excuse for someone else to sin. Certainly, you don't need to cause trouble for yourself. I know in some positions I've been in, members of the congregation would have used knowledge of my depression to cause serious unrest. Pray for wisdom to know how best to share.

But let me urge you: do share your weakness. God created us to live in community. Not shallow community, either.

It gives you the opportunity to share how much you need Jesus. You

---

82. Galatians 4:13–14

are not a saint in the Roman Catholic sense. You are not perfect. You are not sinless. You depend on your Savior every day in a very real and very gritty way. It keeps you from being the Savior but instead the faithful servant.

It allows you to share in the struggles of others as well. So many people around you struggle with depression. Their hollow hearts echo lies, too. You can tell them how you're in the

> *It gives you the opportunity to share how much you need Jesus, to encourage and be encouraged, to take off the mask of "I'm okay."*

trenches with them. Here's what's worked for you. Here's how Jesus is enough. Here are the lies you struggle with; do they struggle with them, too? You can encourage one another!

> It changes everything to know that our own experience of pain can help someone else's. It is, in that sense, redemptive. Despite what some suggest, it is nearly always inappropriate to utter the words 'I know how you feel,' at least without deep exploration and conversation. It is too glib, too dismissive. But if sharing my own story leads someone to recognize that he or she is not the only one, or the first, or the worst—in other words, if my story resonates in some way with another's—then I am profoundly moved to gratitude and hope. I can see that God does have some sort of purpose in it all, that I can be used to help others along the Way. Dare I say it, I can actually begin to see this whole saga as a divine gift.[83]

---

83. Meynell, *When Darkness Seems My Closest Friend,* 172.

It allows your friends the chance to serve and encourage you in a very real way. Do you crave real encouragement? Not useless answers, not theological explanations, but the support of people who have shed the same tears, people who nod in understanding at your wounds, who hold your hands, who hold you up in prayer? That will not happen unless you risk being vulnerable.

It presents a very transparent preaching of the theology of the cross. The theology of the cross says that in my suffering, Christ is given glory. It directly refutes the theology of glory.

It gives you "breathing room" on days when such is necessary. If others understand your struggle, they are more likely to give you room to struggle. If they believe you're just fine, they will expect you to continue to act as if you're just fine. Ah, but if you share your wounds, it may open up room for you to struggle, open up time to treat those wounds.

It also gives you a place to share your struggles honestly. You don't have to put on a mask Sunday morning and pretend to smile. You don't have to "fake it" with the brothers and sisters who you will share eternity with. Don't wallow either, but live honestly.

Given all these positives, I would encourage you to wisely share your depression with those around you. There's no need to advertise, but also no need to hide.

You are known. You are loved. Your Jesus has not abandoned you. You do not need to hide.

Chapter 19

Depression Isn't All Bad

IN MY INFORMAL SURVEY of pastors, I asked how depression affected their ministries. Here are some answers:

- It hurt it, but it didn't destroy it. It's the Lord's church and His call, and He did His work in spite of me, I know. I'm much more reliant on Jesus and less on myself today. Depression does wonders for killing a young pastor's messiah complex. The ministry will be there long after I am gone.

- Helped me to be more authentic. Problems don't happen overnight, and can't be fixed overnight.

- Cancelling of meetings, classes, and shut-ins. Lack of care/concern for contacting delinquents and doing evangelism. High stress times led to impatience and anger with members, especially antagonistic leaders. General lethargy and procrastination.

- It has helped me rely more on God. It has helped me see that the ministry is God's, not mine. It has helped me empathize with the many members of our churches who also struggle with depression. It has humbled me, which is something I drastically needed.

- I think, most people, don't even know that things bother me. Though I have a Care Committee in place, and they know. One is a Counselor and the other a former Public School teacher. They are very helpful. My wife often comments that I need to be more up front and honest with people about things that really, trouble me. Yet, when I do, most people don't seem to have the same concerns (which bugs me even more.)

☐ I spend more and more time in prayer. I think that is a good and important thing.

☐ Negatively: discouraged easily, not working as hard as I could, pessimistic views, "tank" is not filled up so react more negatively more quickly than I should.

☐ Humble, know how much I need the Lord, empathetic with others who struggle emotionally, able to connect with those who struggle

☐ Yes, it taught me to let God be God, to leave his work in his hands and not to try and make it my work. I think it helped me to deal with stress in a more positive manner, spiritually speaking.

☐ Yes, it has affected me when I feel the depression setting in and I simply need to step back and relax. I call these mental health days—I'll go home, sleep, relax and know that this will pass. No—in the sense that it hasn't inhibited my ability to function as pastor (and in most ways, has helped me as a pastor).

☐ Although I hate having it—I have come to see it as a blessing. It helps me to realize my weaknesses and not try to be someone I am not. It has helped me to focus more and more on my Savior for strength. It has also been a blessing for others—as I can truly empathize with those who are suffering depression. I have been there and can understand. The Lord has brought many people into my office for counseling. I have not hidden my struggle with depression and let the people of my congregation know that I struggle with it.[84]

---

84. Italiano, "Depression in the Ministry Survey," all responses are copy-pasted.

I realize that's a long list, but there's a reason I put it all here. I listed both negative and positive reactions to depression in the ministry. If you have depression, I assume you're familiar with many of the negative aspects: procrastination, lethargy, inability to work with others, freezing up under stress, and many others. You've dwelt in the valley of the shadow of death, and you are familiar with its contours. You share these struggles with pastors who also have depression.

> There can be an end to depression. Or perhaps more accurately, you can come to understand depression as a part of you. I don't mean in some sort of hospice sense that death is natural or anything like that. Suffering changes you, whether it is depression, death, persecution, or another form. It does change you. You may receive this change as a gift from our Lord who loves you and seeks to draw you closer to Him. Or you may look at it as a curse and a sign that God doesn't really care. Suffering always creates in us a longing to be free of this earthly life and to join our Lord forever in heaven. This is good. It helps us to understand that this life is transitory, but the Word of the Lord endures forever.[85]

Wait . . . You can see depression as good?

Yes. Yes you can.

I want to encourage you: your depression is a gift.

Did you catch the many times it came up in the list? Allow me to sum up and speak for myself as I do: my depression forces me to lean on God.

I do not know if Paul's thorn in the flesh was depression. More than

---

85. Todd A. Peperkorn, *I Trust When Dark My Road* (St. Louis, MO: The Lutheran Church—Missouri Synod, 2009), 91.

one person spoke to me thinking that it might have been. Whatever it was, we can apply Paul's reaction to his thorn to our reaction to our depression:

> Therefore, to keep me from becoming arrogant due to the extraordinary nature of these revelations, I was given a thorn in my flesh, a messenger of Satan, to torment me, so that I would not become arrogant. Three times I pleaded with the Lord about this, that he would take it away from me. And he said to me, "My grace is sufficient for you, because my power is made perfect in weakness." Therefore I will be glad to boast all the more in my weaknesses, so that the power of Christ may shelter me. That is why I delight in weaknesses, in insults, in hardships, in persecutions, in difficulties, for the sake of Christ. For whenever I am weak, then am I strong.[86]

> [Paul] is unashamed of his weakness. Why? It is because his strength, as well as his identity and purpose, all derive from the security he has discovered in Christ. Christ brings the forgiveness for his guilt, the acceptance that heals his shame, the strength that assuages his insecurities. Paul does not derive his sense of worth, nor understand his identity, from either his role in ministry, or from afflictions and weakness. In short, the thorn keeps him humble, while God's grace frees him from pretense.[87]

I don't need to pretend. God will not love me more if I put on a brave face. He will not love me less if I reveal the broken mess I hide. He knows every crevice tucked away in my hollow heart. He's heard the lies it screams. He knows how much I've believed those lies.

---

86. 2 Corinthians 12:7–10
87. Meynell, *When Darkness Seems My Closest Friend,* 180.

He loves me anyway.

How could I ever hide from one such as him, when he accepts me broken as I am?

I am so, so weak. The morning I wrote the rough draft of this section of the book, I had planned to review the sermon for Sunday, prepare Bible study, and work on this book.

> *You can come to understand depression as a part of you.*

After that, it was off to mow the lawn, visit a shut-in, and make some hospital rounds. After supper, an evening meeting with my education chairman to plan out the coming year. A fairly light day, really, all things concerned.

And then the alarm went off, and I couldn't move. All morning I lay in bed. I hadn't experienced this for years. I had no energy to do anything. The prospect of meeting with anyone was daunting.

And you know what I did? I yelled at myself. "I should know better. I should have this conquered. I've done this before. Come on, Luke. This is stupid. You idiot. You're not under a lot of stress, you've been getting plenty of sleep, you're exercising. No excuse. Get. Out. Of. Bed."

I am not as strong as I think I am.[88]

And it's a lesson I need to learn again and again and again. I am weak. But my hope is not in my strength. My congregation's hope is not in my strength. My members' hope is not in my strength. My strength is so, so small. But where does my help come from? Not from me. Where does their help come from? Not from me.

---

88. Phrasing stolen from Rich Mullins, "We Are Not as Strong as We Think We Are," track 5 on *Songs*, Reunion Records, 1996, compact disc.

My help comes from the Lord, who made heaven and earth.[89]

My depression is a gift. It reminds me how weak I am. It reminds me of all these truths that in my arrogance I forget over and over again. It drives me again and again to Jesus.

I am not enough. Jesus is. He is what I need. I need his grace. I need his forgiveness of my selfish desire to do everything myself. I need his healing in my brokenness. And it is here in my depression that I experience his mercy again and again. "The wound is where the light gets in."[90]

Because Jesus was strong for me, I was free to be weak;
because Jesus won for me, I was free to lose;
because Jesus was someone, I was free to be no one;
because Jesus was extraordinary, I was free to be ordinary;
because Jesus succeeded for me, I was free to fail.[91]

I know that darkness. I know it well. But in the darkness, light shines brightest. And you, walking in darkness, have seen a great light. For to you a child is born. To you a son is given. And the government? It's on his shoulders. Not yours.[92] In your depression, accept your weakness, and see that Jesus is the one who carries you. Lean not on your own understanding. Trust in the Lord.[93] He will not snuff you out like a burning wick. I know you are bruised; he will not break you.[94]

---

89. Psalm 121:1–2

90. Jason Gray, "The Wound is Where the Light Gets In," track 8 on *Where the Light Gets In*, Centricity Music, 2016, MP3.

91. Tullian Tchividjian, *Jesus + Nothing = Everything* (Wheaton, IL: Crossway, 2011), 24.

92. Isaiah 9:2-6

93. Proverbs 3:5

94. Isaiah 42:3

And the only reason I can say this, humanly speaking, is through the blessing of depression. Because I have been broken and healed. Because I am weak. Because my Jesus, your Jesus—he is strong enough. He will shepherd his Church. You are a member of his Church. He will shepherd you.

This is the exact opposite of the theology of glory. It's called the theology of the cross. God uses hardship to draw you to him.

If it weren't for my depression, I would depend so much more on myself. I would not lean on Jesus. I would think I was enough.

I would be wrong.

And so in love, Jesus has allowed me to suffer depression. I have learned how good he is to me, especially because I am not enough. I have learned he is enough. I don't have to pretend. I don't have to smile. I do nothing. He has done everything.

And so I thank Jesus for the blessing of depression. Anything that draws me to him, anything that opens my eyes to his goodness, oh, it is a blessing. Yes, I still suffer. But it is through that suffering that I learn his grace is sufficient for me, too. Even for me.

> *My depression is a gift. It drives me
> again and again to Jesus.*

Chapter 20

Today Is Not the End

TODAY WE STRUGGLE. TODAY we are dragged into darkness and we do not have the strength to fight. Today our hollow hearts echo lies.

Today will end.

A day is coming when you will know not just the muted joy of this world, but true happiness. Your heart will be transformed, and every effect of sin will be taken from you. You will be washed clean of your guilt and shame. Even your depression will flee when the sky rolls back like a cloud and you at last see your Savior face-to-face.

Today seems like it will never end. You know you face such lies, but the truth doesn't seem to break through.

Today will end.

And the tomorrow of endless joy will never end. The lies at last will be silenced. Never again will you be haunted. And Jesus himself will wipe every tear from your eyes.[95]

Your Jesus has not abandoned you. Your Jesus has not let you go. And he will see you through to glory.

---

95. Revelation 21

Today's darkness will end, and the dawn will come.
That is the holy work of homesickness:
to teach our hearts how lonely
they have always been for God.

So let these sighs and tears, Lord Christ, prepare
me for that better gladness that will be mine.
Let all your children learn to grieve well in this
life, knowing we are not just being homesick;
we are letting sorrow carve
the spaces in our souls,
that joy will one day fill.
O Holy Spirit, bless our grief, and
seal our hearts until that day.
Amen.[96]

And the tomorrow of endless joy will never end.

---

96. Douglas Kaine McKelvey, *Every Moment Holy* (Nashville, TN: Rabbit Room Press, 2017), 223.

Devotions for Those with Depression

While the preceding book is meant to give comfort to those who struggle with depression and supply some tools to apply Law and Gospel, sometimes it's good to have something more "bite-size."

These devotions are intended to provide short devotional thoughts to help those who have been diagnosed with depression.

Diagnosis

You know something's wrong. Have you seen the doc yet?

Why not? You afraid of what he'll say?

Or maybe you've already been to the doc, and he's given a name to what you struggle with: depression.

There's something about a diagnosis that can be terrifying. You know that you've struggled for a long time. You know that something isn't clicking the way it should. But to actually name that darkness seems to give it power. It's easier to pretend there's nothing wrong when it doesn't have a name. Once you've got a diagnosis, there's no more pretending.

Diagnosis is necessary. And the diagnosis changes nothing.

Think of the diagnosis as a mirror. All it does is reveal reality. And in that way, it's very much like the Law.

The Law is necessary. The Law reveals our sinful condition. It rips off the mask that leads us to say "I'm pretty okay." Romans 3:20 says, "For this reason, no one will be declared righteous in his sight by works of the law, for through the law we become aware of sin."

Are you frightened by that Law? It cuts, doesn't it? It reveals that I have not served God with all that I am. That I have failed to love my neighbor so, so often. That I am not good enough. I don't serve well enough. I have failed.

But the Law doesn't change anything. It simply reveals reality and makes me deal with it.

Or rather, makes me realize I can't deal with it. I need a Savior.

That Savior has come for you. You're not good enough; he is. And he has dressed you in his robes of righteousness. "But now, completely apart from the law, a righteousness from God has been made known. The Law and the Prophets testify to it. This righteousness from God comes through faith in Jesus Christ to all and over all who believe.

"In fact, there is no difference, because all have sinned and fall short of the glory of God and are justified freely by his grace through the redemption that is in Christ Jesus." (Romans 3:21–24)

So what does that have to do with the fear of your diagnosis?

Just as the diagnosis of the Law doesn't change you, it simply makes you aware of reality, the diagnosis of depression does not change you. It simply makes you aware of the reality.

Jesus dealt with your sin. He knew your darkness. He knew your filth. And he loved you. He said, "I will fight for you." Your depression doesn't change anything for him, either. You are still a loved child of God.

Do not fear this diagnosis. It simply reveals reality.

———

PRAYER: Lord Jesus, I tremble at this word: depression. I fear it. I do not want this word applied to me. Yet, when the only word that applied to me was "sinner," you died for me and gave me a new name: "child of God." Help me cling to this reality as I struggle with this new word, "depression." Hold me tight in your nail-scarred hands as I come to grips with what this word reveals about me. Help me find solace in your unchanging love. Amen.

Fighting the Diagnosis

Have you ever dealt with someone who refused to admit they were sinful? I remember talking to a woman who told me "I'm not sinful. I'm perfect." She refused to admit anything wrong about herself. "I'm thinking positive, so positive things come to me!"

Later on, I heard that she had committed suicide.

Fighting a true diagnosis of sin destroys the soul. The burden of trying to obey the rules is too much for any human. There is a reason Jesus invites, "Come to me all you who are weary and burdened, and I will give you rest. Take my yoke upon you and learn from me, because I am gentle and humble in heart, and you will find rest for your souls. For my yoke is easy and my burden is light." (Matthew 11:28–30)

Why do people fight the diagnosis so much? It boils down to pride, doesn't it? I don't want to admit I need help. But until I discover that desperate need, I will never realize the necessity of the Savior.

If you're struggling with the diagnosis of depression, let me ask you: why?

Is it because you don't want to be weak?

You already admit your weakness regularly, don't you? Do you stand before God and declare "I am by nature sinful. I have sinned against you in thought, word, and deed. I have done what is evil and failed to do what is good"?

I assume you are no hypocrite. I assume you mean those words. I assume you do not merely parrot them for the benefit of looking good or fitting in.

Which means that every single week you're in church, you already admit your desperate need for a Savior. Every week, you openly confess that you are not good enough. And every week you hear those amazing words: you are forgiven. I hope you revel in that forgiveness, because it's for you, too.

Sin is so much worse than depression, isn't it?

So why is it harder for us to admit depression than to admit our sin?

Is it because we think depression is so much worse? How is that possible? What could be worse than rightly earning God's wrath? Or have we fallen for the lie that says some problems of this world damn worse than others?

Is it because we think we need to have it together? Why should we claim to be better than Paul, who admitted his weakness and even gave glory to God for it? (2 Corinthians 12:7–10)

Is it because we fear what will happen to our lives? Nothing has changed. You are not suddenly so much worse just because you have a diagnosis. Your life will not likely swan dive just because the struggles you experience now have a name.

Is it pride that causes you to struggle with that diagnosis?

Confess that pride. You are broken, just like every other human. Your brokenness appears as depression; for someone else, it might appear in some other way. Stop fighting the diagnosis and see it for the blessing it is. It allows you to see the shape of your brokenness and begin dealing with it.

And despite the lies your pride whispers, you are broken. But God loves us in our brokenness, and he himself will repair us.

> In that day I will raise up the fallen shelter of David.
> I will repair the broken parts of its walls,
> and I will raise up its ruins.
> I will rebuild it as in days of old,
> so that they will possess what remains of Edom,
> that is, all the nations who are called by my name,
> declares the LORD, who is doing this. (Amos 9:11–12)

———

PRAYER: Father, I confess my pride. It is so easy to admit sin in general, but hard to admit weakness. Break this proud heart of mine and lean me on you instead. Teach me to rely on you even in this time, even in this diagnosis, and carry me. Amen.

Comfort in Diagnosis

In the last devotion, I urged you to confess your pride, but I didn't really tell you how.

Sinful pride rises up because we fear that we can't depend on anyone else. I would rather depend on me than risk depending on someone who will fail me.

You are forced to be pretty independent much of the time, aren't you? We've all been burned by friends who say they're going to do something and then fail for any number of reasons. We're used to picking up the slack when people don't follow through. We've learned over and over again: we can't depend on other people.

Far too often, we internalize that lesson without ever intending to. We rely on Jesus for the forgiveness of sins, and we praise him for that! But for everything else, we need to pull ourselves up by our bootstraps.

And that's where the pride comes in. I can't depend on anyone else, because they might fail me. So it's my job. I need to be good enough to do it.

And suddenly, there's this diagnosis of depression. Suddenly, I'm being told that I'm not good enough in this area. I want to depend on me, but suddenly . . . I'm not dependable.

I've said it before: This diagnosis changes nothing. It simply forces you to realize you're not strong enough.

Your Jesus is strong enough.

Therefore I will give him an allotment among the great,
and with the strong he will share plunder,
because he poured out his life to death,
and he let himself be counted with rebellious sinners.
He himself carried the sin of many,
and he intercedes for the rebels. (Isaiah 53:12)

He carried the weight of your sins. Every time you failed to love. Every time you thought you were strong enough to carry a burden you were not designed to bear. Every time you hurt your own body because you thought you had to do more. Every sin. Every filth. Every darkness.

If Jesus can carry the weight of your sins, he can carry you.

And not only can he . . . He does. He welcomes you with open arms. He will not drop you. "And this is the will of him who sent me: that I should lose none of those he has given me, but raise them up on the Last Day." (John 6:39)

You can let go of your pride, because you can depend on Jesus. He will not fail you. Even now with this diagnosis, he will not abandon you. There's no slack for you to pick up. He's got it.

Instead of pretending you've got it, depend on Jesus.

———————————

PRAYER: Jesus, forgive me for thinking I have to carry my weight. You bore the weight of my sins, and you carry me now, too. Teach me to depend on you, even now. As I struggle with this diagnosis, remind me of your grace even in depression. Amen.

My Brokenness

"For we know that all of creation is groaning with birth pains right up to the present time." (Romans 8:22)

You have heard this groaning out. You have heard your friends weep through cancer. You have heard the sobs that accompany mourning. You have witnessed natural disasters. Perhaps you've witnessed a childbirth and heard those screams as Eve's curse echoes even today. You are not unfamiliar with the suffering that comes with a broken world.

And now you are broken as well.

Of course, you always knew you were broken. You're very familiar with the contours of sin in your own life. You recognize your own struggles as your sinful flesh hungers for whatever can offend God.

Perhaps you've recognized your own body groaning. As you've aged, maybe you've seen that you can't (or at least shouldn't) play sports with the same verve you used to. Maybe, like me, you've put on far more weight than you ever envisioned in your youth. Maybe you struggle with a physical illness.

And now your mind and heart, also parts of this creation, cry out.

Depression is another symptom of this world's brokenness. It shows that our world is *not right* and forces us to look for something better.

A new creation is coming.

In the world to come, all that is broken will be restored. Your friend weeping over cancer will find joy in a body restored. Those who mourn will laugh in the Dawn that comes. Natural disasters will be no more, as the new heavens and new earth praise God with a united voice. The pains of childbirth will be swallowed up in song.

Every symptom of sin will be gone as Jesus takes his Bride.

And from your brokenness, you will be restored. Your depression will be gone. No more will your heart whisper lies to you. No more will shame claim you. No more will darkness wrap around you.

For Jesus himself has claimed you. He cries out against all your enemies, "This one is mine!"

Today we groan. Tomorrow we rejoice.

"Then I saw a new heaven and a new earth, because the first heaven and the first earth had passed away. And the sea no longer existed. And I saw the Holy City, the New Jerusalem, coming down out of heaven from God, prepared as a bride adorned for her husband.

"And from the throne I heard a loud voice that said, 'Look! God's dwelling is with people. He will dwell with them, and they will be his people. God himself will be with them, and he will be their God. He will wipe away every tear from their eyes. There will be no more death or sorrow or crying or pain, because the former things have passed away.'

"The one who was seated on the throne said to me, 'Look, I am making everything new!' He also said, 'Write, for these words are trustworthy and true.' " (Revelation 21:1–5)

PRAYER: Father, I groan. This weight is too much for me to bear. I know that glory is coming. I long for that day when my depression will vanish like shadows at the coming of the Dawn. Hold me until that day. Do not let me go. Amen.

Today Will End

"But do not forget this one thing, dear friends: For the Lord, one day is like a thousand years, and a thousand years are like one day." (2 Peter 3:8)

And now, as depression takes you, don't you feel like you identify with God? Depression seems to slow everything down, doesn't it? This day feels like a thousand years. And the nights . . . Maybe you can identify with Solomon: "Pain fills all his days. His occupation is frustration. Even at night his heart does not rest. This too is vapor." (Ecclesiastes 2:23)

Depression so often whispers lies. It slows days of torment and hollowness so that every hour feels like an eternity. And in that darkness, it whispers, "This will never end."

Brother, sister, you know the truth: the Dawn is coming, and it is coming so, so soon.

It sure doesn't feel that way, though.

A friend of mine was going through a hard time. He claimed, "God torments us until he takes us to heaven. Life's just going to get worse and worse and worse until I die." Maybe you identify with him. Maybe, if you're going through a depressive episode right now, you agree with him.

It looks like life will just get worse and worse and worse.

Your depression lies.

Yes, this world is broken. Yes, we decay. Yes, we groan.

Today will end.

It's not just the end of time you have to look forward to, though. It's not just heaven. Even here, today, this depressive episode will end.

Today will end.

I won't promise that tomorrow will be better. I don't know that. I don't know what form sin will take tomorrow. I won't promise that your depression will get better. But I promise this: despite how it feels, time continues.

How long did it feel like to Jesus as he wrestled in Gethsemane? For those hours as he struggled in prayer and sweat blood, did it feel like an eternity to an eternal God who had placed himself into time? As he saw those torches crossing the valley toward the Mount of Olives, did every moment last forever?

But time continued. Jesus was arrested. Tried. Crucified. Died. Was buried.

And three days later, he rose.

My friend, today will end. Do not believe the lies of depression. Jesus himself stands with you in this moment. He knows your pain. He has borne your pain. He has taken your darkness and made it his own to release you from it.

Today will end.

———

PRAYER: When will it end, Father? When will I be able to feel again? When will I be able to smile? I want to rejoice in your grace, but all I can do is weep. Hold me now. Carry me through this endless moment. Wrap my fingers around the knowledge that today will end, that even this time is in your hands. You have not forgotten me. Carry me now. Amen.

How Long, O Lord?

It's okay to not be okay.

Maybe you've heard that before. Maybe you've laughed at it. Maybe you've shrugged at it. Whatever your reaction, I want you to know: it's true.

David cried out to the Lord:

How long, O LORD? Will you forget me forever?
How long will you hide your face from me?
How long must I experience worries in my soul,
sorrow in my heart every day?
How long will my enemy tower over me? (Psalm 13:1–2)

He wrestled with his thoughts . . . even as you wrestle with yours. He experienced sorrow in his heart, even as you do.

He didn't keep it in. He didn't say, "I'll get over this." He didn't pretend everything was okay. He cried out to God.

Don't pretend everything is okay when you struggle through a depressive episode. Cry out to God. He knows your heart. He will not be shocked at what is going on inside of you. Take it to the Lord in prayer.

Look on me and answer, O LORD my God.
Give light to my eyes,
so I do not sleep in death,
so my enemy does not say, "I have overcome him,"
so my foes do not rejoice when I fall. (Psalm 13:3–4)

Maybe it doesn't sound very Christian to say . . . but David, a man after God's own heart, said it.

It's okay to not be okay.

But even in his distress, even as David cries out to God, hear his confidence:

> But I trust in your mercy.
> My heart rejoices in your salvation.
> I will sing to the LORD,
>   because he has accomplished his purpose for me. (Psalm 13:5–6)

Even now, David trusts in God's love. Even as he feels that God has forgotten him, he knows the truth: God's love has not failed. It cannot fail. It will not fail. Even now, when it feels as if God has hidden his face, David rejoices in God's salvation. Even in this pit, he will sing to the Lord.

Admitting your struggle does not make you unfaithful. Confessing your depression does not make you unworthy to be a child of God.

It means that you know your weakness and you turn to God for rescue, like a child confident that their parent will answer.

So when the darkness comes, cry out. Your God's love will not fail you. You may not feel him, but he has not abandoned you. He has not turned his face from you. You are not being petty as you pray for yourself. You are not being unfaithful as you struggle with this brokenness.

Let me encourage you: Use Psalm 13. Pray it. Let it give voice to your grief.

But do not forget those last verses. Even now, even in the darkness, God's love does not fail you. He has not forgotten you. He has already saved you.

PRAYER: How long will you forget me, O God? Open my mouth to give voice to my cry. You know my grief. You know my struggle. Lord, I offer it up to you. Take all that I am. I trust your unfailing love; remind me of that unfailing love now. Do not forget me. Amen.

Coping

One pastor suggested to me that Noah planted a vineyard and got drunk because he needed to cope with a dead world. Clearly, we could argue a lot about why Noah did what he did, but I know plenty of people who cope with difficult lives by turning to alcohol.

In your depression, alcohol might call out to you. Maybe it's not alcohol. Maybe it's some other substance that can dull pain. It can make you set aside your cares for a while.

Depending on alcohol or any other substance is a sin.

If you have turned to a substance to cope with your depression, please stop. And yes, even get help. Drunkenness is a serious sin. "And do not get drunk on wine, which causes you to lose control. Instead, be filled with the Spirit." (Ephesians 5:18)

This substance will not help you. It may dull your struggle for a short time, but it will end up causing more trouble. It will depress you further. It will cause harm to those closest to you. I understand that it calls to you, and you are desperate for relief from somewhere, anywhere. I understand your struggle. I understand wanting to just sit down and let it roll over you and away. I understand trying to find a solution in a bottle.

So trust me when I say: this is not the place to find relief.

LORD, hear my prayer.
Give ear to my cry for mercy.
In your faithfulness, answer me in your righteousness. (Psalm 143:1)

Alcohol will not save you. No substance can. I know you know that, but we do not always act in line with what we know. If you've turned to alcohol or any substance as the source of your relief, turn to the Lord and confess. You have replaced the Creator with a creation. Admit your sin.

Relief does not come from alcohol. It comes from no substance. Relief only comes from the Lord.

And he sends you real relief: Forgiveness. Real forgiveness; not pretend forgiveness for pretend sin, but real forgiveness for real sin. Jesus died also for you, and also for this sin.

Alcohol will not be faithful to you. No substance will lift you up. These things give no righteousness. But God in his faithfulness comes to you. God in his righteousness clothes you. You do not need the alcohol to cope. God provides what you need.

Now I encourage you: find help. Do not hide this sin and pretend you can defeat it by yourself. Do not think you can drown these demons alone. God is good to you; he has surrounded you with fellow believers who desperately need Jesus, just as you do. Who mourn and struggle together, just as you do. Who can point you to Jesus.

And Jesus provides exactly what's needed: relief.

PRAYER: Lord, I confess that in my depression, in my brokenness, I have sought to find relief in alcohol. I confess that I am not strong enough. Lord, take my sins. Keep your promise to me and make me new. Give me strength to find help and encouragement in my struggle. Keep your cross before my eyes always. Amen.

Be Still

Depression does not allow me to get anything done. When it strikes me, I achieve nothing on my to-do list. I hate it. Depression drives me to sit still, accomplishing nothing and feeling more and more guilty. I know what I should do. I know that as a pastor I am required to complete certain tasks. And why am I not doing it?

Because. That's all.

This shames me, and I struggle all the more to get things done, and I still accomplish nothing. It's this constant cycle of shame, lethargy, and more shame.

Be still.

Your God knows what you need. He knows what your family needs. And your God will provide. Yes, sometimes he provides through you. But he also knows your depression, and he can and will provide what is needed through others.

"Be still, and know that I am God." (Psalm 46:10) And do you know how that psalm goes? "The LORD of Armies is with us. / The God of Jacob is a fortress for us."

Your fortress is not what you do. Your fortress is not your service to others. Your fortress is not being busy or accomplishing everything on your to-do list. These things will not protect you. You do not have to complete these things to be safe.

The Lord is your fortress. He protects you. And do you know what you have to do to be safe in a fortress?

Just be still.

When those days come, be still. Turn on some good music that will point you to God's faithfulness to you. Perhaps read some if you can muster the energy. And don't read the deep things that will tax your intellect; read some sweet reminders of the Gospel. Take a rest; God has what you require.

"But what about all those things that have to get done?" you say.

I know. Trust me, I know! There's always more, isn't there? Is God your fortress only when everything's put together?

Long-term? Perhaps it's time to let some things go.

Short-term? Cancel a meeting. It won't be the end of the world. Reschedule. It's okay. Figure out what *must* happen and focus on just that.

Practically speaking, I'd recommend getting ahead a few weeks where you can. That way, when these days come, you can take the day off.

But in all this, remember who your fortress is. Be still. God is God. He's got you covered. Yes, even you.

PRAYER: Lord, I am so tired, and there is so much yet to do. Help me to trust you more. Use me as you would, and remind me that you are my fortress. Keep me safe. Teach me how to be still. Amen.

Shame

I know you want to hide it. You have this darkness inside of you. I'm not even talking about your depression. There is this thing that you are ashamed of. Maybe it's something you did long ago. Maybe it's a habit you've tried to break for years, maybe decades. You know it's wrong, and yet it enslaves you.

Your depression takes that darkness and shoves your face in it. "Look at this!" it screams. "You call yourself a Christian? How could you claim that title when you do this?"

The shame strikes and sinks into your skin and your heart and weighs you down. You hide.

Jesus knows what you have done.

And he is not ashamed.

"For he who sanctifies and those who are being sanctified all have one Father. For that reason, he is not ashamed to call them brothers." (Hebrews 2:11) Jesus is not ashamed to call *you* his brother, his sister. He sanctifies you. He makes you holy. He claims you as his own.

Your depression tells you that you are worse. You may know in your head that your sin is no worse than any other's. You may know that you are forgiven. But the depression rushes in and tries to smother that knowledge.

Don't believe that lie.

Whatever darkness your depression shames you over, Jesus knows and has forgiven it. He is not ashamed of you.

Whatever darkness you struggle with now and try to keep secret out of shame, your temptation is common. And Jesus himself faced that temptation. He didn't do it to shame you. He didn't do it to show you "how easy it is." He did it to free you. He faced it and defeated it to give you his victory.

He didn't roll his eyes that he had to do it. He chose you, before the foundation of the world, knowing fully all there is to know about you.

And now you are forgiven.

Jesus himself stands beside you and declares, "This is my brother! This is my sister! This one is mine! I won't look away from him, and I won't turn my head. I know everything there is to know about him. He can't scare me away! I have paid for her with my blood, and no one can take her from my hand!"

I understand shame. I know what those lies whisper.

They are lies.

Jesus is not ashamed of you.

———————

PRAYER: Jesus, I want to hide. I know my sin. It strangles me. And yet, it still calls to me, and I want to go to it. Help me, Lord. Help me fight this temptation. You tell me you are not ashamed, even when I struggle with *this*. Take my sin now. Wash me. Make me new. Speak the truth to me when my depression lies. Amen.

For the Joy Set Before

When I'm in the midst of a depressive episode, I hate hearing that Jesus loves me.

"Well, of course he loves me. He has to. I'm part of the world. He loves everyone. Big deal. He shouldn't love me. I don't have anything to offer him. If he got to pick and choose, he wouldn't choose me to love."

Does that sound familiar?

Depression can offer the worst deception because there's a tiny nugget of truth in it. The whispers are right when they say you offer nothing to God. At least nothing he needs. And it's not like you can pay for any of your sins. And in that, you are the same as every other human who has ever lived. The only thing we bring to the table in salvation is our sin.

But Jesus has never loved you because of something you offer him. He has never loved you because of your accomplishments. He has never loved you because you fought against sin or spoke the Gospel boldly.

Jesus loves you . . . because he loves you.

And Jesus doesn't wrinkle his nose and look at you and say, "Well, fine, you can come, too." Listen: "And let us run with perseverance the race marked out for us, fixing our eyes on Jesus, the pioneer and perfecter of faith. For the joy set before him he endured the cross, scorning its shame, and sat down at the right hand of the throne of God." (Hebrews 12:1–2 NIV)

Did you see that?

Not because he had to. Not because the world was a package deal. Not because it was simply the right thing to do.

"For the joy set before him."

Jesus looks at you, and he says, "For the joy of having you in my Kingdom, for the joy of you being mine, for the joy of claiming you as my own, I will endure the cross. I scorn its shame. I sit down at the right hand of my Father. And all this because I want to make you mine. I rejoice to make you mine."

Do you see? He doesn't look at his nail-scarred hands and think it a waste. He looks at you and says, "Worth it." Claiming you is a source of joy for Jesus.

So when your depression whispers deceptions to you, focus on Jesus. Fix your eyes on your Savior. For joy he claimed you. For joy he paid for you. He rejoices to name you his.

———

PRAYER: Sometimes your love hurts, Lord. I know I am not worth it. And still you reach out your hands in forgiveness and joy. Now, in my depression, keep your joy and hold me tight. Help me see that you have paid for me in joy. Amen.

That I Should Lose None

Depression threatens to tear me from Jesus. It pries my fingers one by one from his cross. It hollows out my heart so there is no love left for my neighbor nor for God. I cannot hold on anymore. I am so, so tired of fighting.

Do you feel that way? You know the darkness cannot smother Jesus, but it can smother you so easily.

You know this truth already, but let me remind you: Your salvation does not depend on you. It does not depend on your ability to "hang on." It does not depend on your ability to look like you have it all together. It does not depend on your ability to serve.

It depends on Jesus.

I know it feels like you walk through the valley of the shadow of death. I know it feels like the walls are closing in and the sun has been swallowed in a starless sky. I know you cannot find your way.

Do not fear. Your Shepherd has walked this path before. He walked ahead of you, carrying your burdens. He passed through this valley and died on a cross for you. For *you*. And after that death, he emerged from this dark valley to sunlit meadows beyond.

And now he walks beside you. He is here in this dark valley with you. Do you hear his promise? "And this is the will of him who sent me: that I should lose none of those he has given me, but raise them up on the Last Day." (John 6:39)

Your strength will not save you. Jesus's strength already has.

You cannot hold on. You do not have the strength. It's okay. Rest. It doesn't depend on you.

With his nail-scarred hands Jesus has saved you. And if that is how it started, well, that is how it continues. Jesus has you, and your darkness cannot scare him away. In fact, he shines like a light in your darkness. But even if you cannot see him, he is here.

And let me give you one more encouragement. Your heart is weak. It condemns you. But Jesus is greater than your heart. "This is how we know that we are of the truth and how we will set our hearts at rest in his presence: If our hearts condemn us, God is greater than our hearts, and he knows everything." (1 John 3:19–20)

Once again, it doesn't depend on you or your strength. It depends on Jesus. And he will lose none.

You're in good hands.

———

PRAYER: Lord, I am so weak. I cannot hold on to you. Hold on to me. Keep your promise. When all I see is darkness, be my Light. When all I experience is pain, be my Healing. When all I am is weak, be my Strength. Hold me until I see you face-to-face. Amen.

Works Cited

American Foundation for Suicide Prevention. "Suicide Statistics." Accessed June 25, 2018. https://afsp.org/about-suicide/suicide-statistics/.

Anonymous. "I once tried to explain depression." Facebook, Accessed April 8, 2018.

Anxiety and Depression Association of America. "Facts and Statistics." Accessed June 25, 2018. https://adaa.org/about-adaa/press-room/facts-statistics.

Archer, Dale. "Vitamin D Deficiency and Depression." Psychology Today. July 11, 2013. https://www.psychologytoday.com/us/blog/reading-between-the-headlines/201307/vitamin-d-deficiency-and-depression.

Floysvik, Ingvar. *When God Becomes My Enemy.* Saint Louis, MO: Concordia Academic Press, 1997.

Gray, Jason. "The Wound is Where the Light Gets In." Track 8 on *Where the Light Gets In.* Centricity Music, 2016, MP3.

Harvard Health. "What Causes Depression?" Last modified January 10, 2022. https://www.health.harvard.edu/mind-and-mood/what-causes-depression.

Italiano, Luke. "Depression in the Ministry Survey." Conducted in March–April 2018. (Respondents' answers are listed anonymously.)

Luther, Martin, and David P. Kuske. *Luther's Catechism: The Small Catechism of Dr. Martin Luther and an Exposition for Children and Adults Written in Contemporary English*. Milwaukee, WI: Northwestern Publishing House, 1989.

Manning, Brennan. *The Ragamuffin Gospel*. Sisters, OR: Multnomah Publishers, 2000.

Mayo Clinic Staff. "Depression (major depressive disorder)." Mayo Clinic. Feb. 3, 2018. https://www.mayoclinic.org/diseases-conditions/depression/symptoms-causes/syc-20356007.

McKelvey, Douglas Kaine. *Every Moment Holy*. Nashville, TN: Rabbit Room Press, 2017.

Meynell, Mark. *When Darkness Seems My Closest Friend*. London: Inter-Varsity Press, 2018.

Mullins, Rich. *Rich Mullins: Home*. Nashville, TN: VoxCorp, 1998.

Mullins, Rich. "We Are Not as Strong as We Think We Are." Track 5 on *Songs*. Reunion Records, 1996, compact disc.

Peperkorn, Todd A. *I Trust When Dark My Road*. St. Louis, MO: The Lutheran Church—Missouri Synod, 2009.

Peterson, Andrew. "Be Kind to Yourself." Track 8 on *The Burning Edge of Dawn*. Centricity Music, 2015. MP3.

Reynolds, Rebecca K. *Courage, Dear Heart*. Colorado Springs, CO: NavPress, 2018.

Saunders, Stephen M. *A Christian Guide to Mental Illness, Volume 1.* Milwaukee, WI: Northwestern Publishing House, 2016.

Tchividjian, Tullian. *Jesus + Nothing = Everything.* Wheaton, IL: Crossway, 2011.

Veith, Gene Edward Jr. *The Spirituality of the Cross.* St. Louis, MO: Concordia Publishing House, 1999.

Wilson, Jared C. *The Pastor's Justification.* Wheaton, IL: Crossway, 2013.

Recommended
Reading

Several books greatly helped me in my depression. Others I wish I had when my depression was at its worst. Not everything in these books is solid; I'm not recommending them because of every part of their doctrinal content. Yet their phrasings of the Gospel and the comfort it brings helped me.

You'll notice that not every book directly addresses depression. Not everything had to be aimed at depression to be helpful to me. If something spoke of the Gospel in a way that touched my heart, if it brought healing to my sin-weary soul, it also eased my depression. If you struggle with depression or want to offer something to a friend struggling with depression, you could do far worse than looking these books up.

———————

Boundaries by Henry Cloud and John Townsend—
> While not a book addressing depression in any direct way, this volume helped me immensely in dealing with the lies my depression spoke to me. I had gotten extremely close to a church member family. When the family fell apart, they dragged me deep into the darkness of depression. *Boundaries* helped me grasp that there was a separation between me and them. If you find yourself

too tied emotionally to those around you, this book may be of service to you. It is also highly useful for those who have a hard time saying "no." If this one isn't on your shelf, get it!

Every Moment Holy by Douglas Kaine McKelvey—
> If poetry touches you, this collection of prayers and brief liturgies may be of great service. McKelvey gives voice to the struggles of Christians with exquisite vocabulary. Light on objective justification, the statement that Jesus has saved you, period, I would never recommend this book alone, but it could be very useful in putting together prayers that express the struggle the believer is going through while in a dark place. The end of my paper quoted his prayer entitled "A Liturgy for an Inconsolable Homesickness."

When Darkness Seems My Closest Friend by Mark Meynell—
> I wish I'd had this book when I first began struggling with depression. Meynell speaks specifically about his ministry and how depression interacted with it. It could be a touchstone for realizing that you are not alone, particularly if you are a church leader. The recommended reading and recommended listening sections in the back alone are worth the price of the book.

I Trust When Dark My Road: A Lutheran View of Depression by Todd A. Peperkorn—
> This book was recommended to me when I was going through the worst of my depression, but I didn't read it until I prepared this book. That was foolish of me! Peperkorn is a Lutheran pastor who faced severe depression and even planned suicide. This thin book tells his story. It's available for free at https://www.lcms.org/document.fdoc?src=lcm&id=721, so you have no excuse to not pick it up!

Courage, Dear Heart: Letters to a Weary World by Rebecca K. Reynolds—

If you struggle with depression, the letters in this book may give a voice to your suffering. It offers some real comfort as well, pointing to Christ. Unlike the other books on this list, *Courage, Dear Heart* focuses more on single emotions: rejected, abused, homesick, and the like. The back of the book tells you the tone: "The world is broken. I am broken. And my need is dire." If that quotation calls to you, this book is well worth your time.

Jesus + Nothing = Everything by Tullian Tchividjian—

Tchividjian's ministry was falling apart when he rediscovered the Gospel. This book takes the reader through the wonders of the Gospel in a fantastic way. While not addressing depression directly, it helped me grasp the Gospel *for me* in much more concrete terms.

About the Author

Luke Italiano has served as a pastor since 2011. He also wears the names husband, father, brother, friend, and many more. But over all these, he is blessed to be called "Child of God." Joyfully serving the Savior who loves him, even in his brokenness. Sharing that good news with others in their brokenness. And rejoicing in the promise of a perfect heavenly home to come.

Dawnsbrook

dawnsbrook.com

 https://www.facebook.com/DawnsbrookPress
https://www.instagram.com/dawnsbrookpress/